TWAYNE'S WORLD AUTHORS SERIES

A Survey of the World's Literature

Sylvia Bowman, Indiana University

GENERAL EDITOR

SPAIN

Gerald E. Wade, Vanderbilt University
Janet W. Diaz, University of North Carolina

EDITORS

The Contemporary Spanish Theater
(1949-1972)

TWAS 336

The Contemporary Spanish Theater (1949-1972)

By MARION P. HOLT

*Staten Island Community College,
City University of New York*

TWAYNE PUBLISHERS

A DIVISION OF G. K. HALL & CO., BOSTON

Library of Congress Cataloging in Publication Data

Holt, Marion P
  The contemporary Spanish theater (1949-1972)

  (Twayne's world author series, TWAS 336. Spain)
  Bibliography: p. 177-80.
  1. Spanish drama—20th century—History and criticism. I.
Title.
PQ6115.H65   862'.6'409   74-12472
ISBN 0-8057-2243-2

MANUFACTURED IN THE UNITED STATES OF AMERICA

DEDICATED TO THE MEMORY OF HAZEL ABBOTT
AND HER THEATER

Contents

About the Author

Marion P. Holt holds the A.B. degree in Modern Languages from Wofford College and the Ph.D. in Spanish from the University of Illinois. He has taught courses in Spanish language and literature and in comparative literature at Converse College, Queens College (CUNY), and the University of Missouri-St. Louis. He is presently Professor of Modern Languages at Staten Island Community College of CUNY where he conducts an internship program in Spanish theater. His principal area of scholarly and professional interest has been the twentieth-century drama of Spain and other European countries. Among his publications are college text editions of López Rubio's *La venda en los ojos* and Ruiz Iriarte's *El carrusell* and *The Modern Spanish Stage: Four Plays*, an anthology of plays in English translation by Buero-Vallejo, Sastre, López Rubio, and Casona.

Preface

The contemporary theater of Spain is largely unknown in the English-speaking world beyond the confines of departments of Hispanic studies in colleges and universities. Although three recent studies are now available—Farris Anderson's *Alfonso Sastre* (1971), Joelyn Ruple's *Antonio Buero Vallejo: The First Fifteen Years* (1971), and Martha T. Halsey's *Antonio Buero Vallejo* (1973)—no inclusive investigation in the area of post-civil war Spanish drama has been published in English. Of the numerous Spanish dramatists of the last two decades, only Buero and Sastre have achieved a degree of critical recognition outside their homeland. While the efforts of these two writers have provided a direction and a basis for the revitalization of the modern Spanish stage, their works represent only a small part of the total dramatic output in Spain in the second half of the twentieth century. Indeed, the number of new works produced in Madrid each year compares with or exceeds those originating in other major European capitals. In 1971 there were more than thirty theaters in Madrid used exclusively for the presentation of live drama.

There has been a tendency in the academic world to treat Spain's modern theater as a phenomenon occurring in extreme isolation and as an aspect of artistic creativity almost totally neutralized by censorship. However, in spite of inhibiting conditions peculiar to Spain, especially those resulting from the aftereffects of the civil war of 1936-39, the oft-lamented "crises" of the Spanish theater have been more often than not closely related to the problems which confront writers, directors, and producers in other Western countries. Any truly objective investigation can only lead to the conclusion that a number of plays written in Spain since 1949 would have found their way to the professional and nonprofessional stages of other nations had adequate translations and critical attention been forthcoming. It is indeed unfortunate that so many viable theatrical works have been relegated to the shelves of libraries during the lifetimes of their creators.

Although scholarly investigation of the postwar Spanish drama has long received encouragement from such prominent Hispanists as William Shoemaker and Gerald Wade, studies of contemporary peninsular playwrights were rare before 1965. Interest has increased notably in recent years, as evidenced by the number of doctoral dissertations completed or in progress and the frequency with which new articles on the Spanish theater are appearing. George Wellwarth's enthusiastic sponsorship of the so-called underground playwrights of the 1960's has focused attention on a group of Spanish writers whose commitment to a new mode of dramatic expression might otherwise have gone unnoticed.

It is the intent of this book to introduce to the general English-speaking public a significant body of contemporary dramatic writing as well as to provide a concise survey of developments in the Spanish theater since 1949 for the student and professional in the fields of theater and twentieth-century literature in general. It is hoped that this presentation will help to remedy what might be called the "predicament" of living Spanish playwrights whose work has received far less recognition and dissemination than it merits—a neglect resulting from political attitudes as well as from the lack of translations and the indifference or insulation of many critics. The study deals essentially with plays written in Spain since 1949—a year which has no special social or political associations but which clearly marks the beginning of a period of creative revitalization in Spanish theatrical affairs.

The publication of significant new dramatic writing in the theater journal *Primer Acto* and the early appearance of a wide selection of plays in the series entitled *Colección teatro* (published by Escelicer in Madrid) have made it possible to consider works first performed as recently as the spring season of 1972. The record of all aspects of theatrical activity in Spain included in Sainz de Robles's yearly anthology of representative plays of each season since 1949-50 has been invaluable for the purpose of documentation. Where unpublished plays are discussed, the source of the manuscript or of information on the work in question is indicated in the "Notes and References."

Because of considerations of space, and the scope of material to be covered, certain limitations have been necessary. Although Buero-Vallejo and Sastre, by any criteria, stand large in the Spanish theater since 1949, the space devoted to them may seem somewhat less than their importance would dictate. However, Farris Anderson's excellent and detailed presentation of Sastre's plays and critical writings is available to the interested reader and is unlikely to be surpassed; Joelyn Ruple's highly readable study of Buero provides a fine introduction to that playwright's work; and Martha Halsey's recent book offers an even more detailed account of Buero's career to date. No special section is devoted to the contributions of the significant but marginal "underground" writers since their work has been well documented and analyzed by Wellwarth in his *Spanish Underground Drama.*

For chronological reasons the plays of Enrique Jardiel Poncela have been excluded. The première of the last completed work by Jardiel took place at the beginning of 1949, and although this innovative and talented dramatist's influence is obvious in the comic theater of the 1950's, his years of creative activity do not fall within the period under consideration here. Alejandro Casona's great popularity in Madrid after 1962 was based principally on plays written many years before while he was living in Mexico and Argentina. For this reason no detailed presentation of his theater has been attempted in the present study. But these exclusions in no sense indicate a lack of recognition of the special contributions of both dramatists in their own time to a continuation of the Spanish theatrical tradition.

Where a particular author and specific plays have been singled out for analysis, the choice has been my own in all cases, but the critical opinions of other observers of the contemporary theatrical scene have been weighed in the selection. Since only a few post-war plays exist in English versions, fairly detailed descriptions of the action, plot, and characters of one or more representative or outstanding works of several playwrights are supplied; pertinent and representative sections of dialogue are also included in some instances. All translations of titles of works not available in English and passages of dialogue—except for those otherwise indicated in notes—are my own. Quotations from books, articles, and reviews written in Spanish have also been translated for the benefit of the general reader.

The plays of all dramatists discussed in this book are covered by international copyright. Inquiries concerning performance should be directed to the Sociedad General de Autores de España, Madrid. Permissions for performance of the plays of Antonio Buero-Vallejo in the English-speaking world must be obtained from Hope Leresche & Steele, 11 Jubilee Place, London SW3.

MARION P. HOLT

New York, N.Y.

Chronology

1949 Premiere of *Los tigres escondidos en la alcoba* (The Tigers Hidden in the Bedroom), the last play of Enrique Jardiel Poncela.

Premier of *Alberto,* marking return of José López Rubio to ranks of Spanish playwrights.

First performance of *Historia de una escalera* (Story of a Stairway), first Lope de Vega Prize award since end of Civil War and first produced play of Antonio Buero-Vallejo.

1950 Premiere of Victor Ruiz Iriarte's *El landó de seis caballos* (The Six-Horse Landau).

1952 Death of Enrique Jardiel Poncela.

Premiere of Edgar Neville's *El baile* (The Dance).

First presentation of *Tres sombreros de copa* (Three Top Hats), marking beginning of Miguel Mihura's career as an independent playwright.

1953 Performance of Alfonso Sastre's *Escuadra hacia la muerte* (Condemned Squad) by Teatro Popular Universitario.

1954 Death of Jacinto Benavente.

Premiere of Joaquin Calvo-Sotelo's *La muralla* (The Wall).

1955 Premiere of *Telarañas* (Cobwebs), first play of Carlos Muñiz.

1957 Publication of *Primer Acto* begins.

1958 Premiere of *Un soñador para un pueblo* (A Dreamer for a People), first in the cycle of historical plays by Buero-Vallejo.

1959 First staging of *El teatrito de Don Ramón* (Don Ramon's Small Theater) by José Martín Recuerda, Lope de Vega Prize winner for 1958.

1960 Premiere of Ricardo Rodríguez Buded's *Un hombre duerme* (A Man is Sleeping).

1962 First performance of Lauro Olmo's *La camisa* (The Shirt).

Return of Alejandro Casona to Spain for Madrid premiere of *La dama del alba* (Lady of the Dawn).

1963 Premiere of Antonio Gala's *Los verdes campos del Edén* (The Green Fields of Eden).

1965 Death of Alejandro Casona.

1968 Death of Edgar Neville.

1969 Opening of the Lady Pepa, first of the cafés-teatro.

1970 Death of Carlos Llopis.

Publication of *Teatro difícil*, works of Jorge Díaz, A. Martínez Ballesteros, José Ruibal, and others, staged by Teatro-club Pueblo.

1971 Premiere of Buero-Vallejo's *La llegada de los dioses* (The Arrival of the Gods).

1972 Election of Buero-Vallejo to the Real Academia Española.

CHAPTER 1

Introduction

I *The State of the Spanish Theater in 1939*

A T the end of the civil war of 1936-39, theatrical production resumed in Madrid within days after the fall of the capital to the Nationalist forces. But the artistic community had been devastated by a tragic conflict. Valle-Inclán had died shortly before the beginning of hostilities; García Lorca had been murdered by a mob in Granada; Casona had chosen exile in Spanish America; and the generation of young playwrights that had promised a renewal of the dramatic impulse in Spain at the end of the decade of the 1920's and during the early years of the Republic, had dispersed. Benavente, Nobel Prize winner and the dominant Spanish dramatic writer of the first quarter of the twentieth century, had shown ambivalent political sentiments during the war, but the new government permitted his return to Madrid from Valencia in 1939. He quickly resumed his career, writing steadily until his death in 1952.[1]

Most of the other dramatic works presented in Spain in the years immediately following the war were the products of established playwrights of the older generation or of a few younger writers whose efforts did not offend the regime either because they gave ideological support to traditional values (in the case of Pemán) or because they represented an aesthetic concept removed from political or religious considerations. Of the younger playwrights of the prewar generation, only Enrique Jardiel Poncela produced works of a quality that enables them to survive critical scrutiny today.[2] Obviously, the imposed censorship, the economic stagnation of the nation, and the conservative tastes of most of the theater public—as well as the caution of producers and impresarios—were formidable obstacles to experimentation in form or the presentation of provocative themes on the stage.

As World War II continued in Europe and Asia, Spain's theater reflected the official neutrality of the Spanish government. In

15

France, England, Germany, and Italy the effects of the war or of military occupation made serious theatrical production difficult or impossible. But even in the United States, which was spared the devastation of bombings and invasion, the theater of those years was generally commonplace, with a generous sampling of patriotically slanted drama and musical comedy balanced by suspense plays and situation comedies sketched in conventional format.

II *The First Postwar Spanish Dramatists*

Inevitably, a new generation of aspiring playwrights did appear in Spain, though few achieved productions of their works prior to 1949. Víctor Ruiz Iriarte (b. 1912) was the first truly promising new writer to join the ranks of performed dramatists. He revealed a sensitive mind and skill for dramatic effect in *El puente de los suicidas* (Suicide Bridge) in 1944, and two years later he was awarded the Piquer Prize of the Real Academia Española for *Academia de amor* (School for Love). With plays such as *El landó de seis caballos* (The Six-Horse Landau, 1950), and *El pobrecito embustero* (The Poor Deceiver, 1953), Ruiz Iriarte developed a style and aesthetic approach—characterized by both sentimentality and a pronounced Pirandellian view of dramatic structure—that were recognizably his own. Although many of his most popular and successful plays have been farces or comedies with serious undertones, the most consummate efforts of his mature years have been the serious dramas *La señora recibe una carta* (A Letter Comes, 1967) and *Historia de un adulterio* (Story of a Deceit, 1970).

Carlos Llopis (1915-1970), a young actor-turned-playwright whose first play had appeared shortly before the end of the civil war, demonstrated a talent for humoristic writing that was far from pedestrian in *Ni Margarita, ni el diablo* (Neither Margarita nor The Devil, 1943) and *Lo que no dijo Guillermo* (What William Didn't Say, 1947) and in several other early comedies. Carlos Llopis was overshadowed at first by Jardiel Poncela and later by Mihura, but for more than two decades his name was a familiar one to theater audiences in Madrid.

It was not until the premiere of *Historia de una escalera* (Story of a Stairway) in 1949 that a new dramatist created a genuine wave of excitement in Madrid. Antonio Buero-Vallejo (b. 1916) was totally unknown to the judges who awarded him the Lope de Vega Prize for what was actually his third full-length play, but the dramatic superiority of his entry was unmistakable.[3] Buero's *Story of a Stairway* had an impact in Spain comparable to that achieved by Tennessee Williams only four years earlier in the United States with *The Glass Menagerie,* and by Arthur Miller in 1949 with *Death of a Salesman.* Describing the opening night of the play for *Insula,* Arturo del Hoyo wrote: "From the first moments of the performance the spectator was aware that *Story of a Stairway,* with its sense of dramatic values, was what had been needed in our theater to help it free itself from paralysis, from mediocrity. For since 1939 the Spanish theater had been living among the ruins of the past."[4] If the plays of Buero that followed in the next few years were less widely admired than his first, they in no way altered the critical judgment given in 1949: his was a major dramatic talent. With the cycle of historical dramas that he began in 1958, with *El tragaluz* (Basement Skylight, 1967) and a fourth historical play, *El sueño de la razón* (The Sleep of Reason, 1970), Buero's dominant position in the Spanish theater of the second half of the twentieth century was firmly established.

Experimental drama was being attempted in the universities in the 1940's, and two very dissimilar young men, Alfonso Sastre (b. 1926) and Alfonso Paso (b. 1926), whose names would become familiar to every theatergoer in the next decade, were writing their first plays, mainly short works in collaboration with others in an enthusiastic group that proclaimed their rejection of the theatrical establishment and its stagnation. Sastre was composing tracts *about* theater and its purposes even before his own plays began to be performed and discussed. He first attracted special attention with his articles on drama and with a manifesto prepared with the critic José María de Quinto in which the establishment of a Theater of Social Protest was urged. His open statements calling for the abolishment of precensorship eventually made him a symbol of opposition to all outside controls over theatrical production.

Sastre's career as a dramatist can be said to have begun in earnest with the performances of his *Escuadra hacia la muerte* (Condemned Squad) given by the Teatro Popular Universitario in March, 1953, in the state-supported María Guerrero Theater.

After the third performance, *Condemned Squad* was closed by the authorities, but the impression made by the event could not be erased. The following year, Sastre's *La mordaza* (The Gag) was given a professional staging, and *La sangre de Dios* (The Blood of God) was produced in Valencia in 1955. However, several of the plays he wrote in this period ran into difficulties with the censors, and even though these "forbidden" works were eventually published and circulated in Spain, they have yet to be performed. Since 1960 only three new plays by Sastre have been staged in Madrid, and his most ambitious works remain unperformed.[5] Sastre has been called "Spain's boldest innovator,"[6] and, although his plays have been seen on the stage less frequently than those of Buero, his agitation for a theater of social consequence has made him a major force in the development of Spain's contemporary drama.

Alfonso Paso, the early associate of Sastre in their university days and now Spain's most prolific and successful playwright (in terms of box-office appeal), was born into a theatrical family and enjoyed close contact with the stage from childhood. Several short works of his, written independently of, or in collaboration with, other members of the vanguard theater group known as *Arte Nuevo,* were performed between 1946 and 1952, and in 1953 Alfonso Paso moved into the professional arena with two full-length comedies, *No se dice adiós, sino hasta luego* (One doesn't Say Goodbye but See you Later) and *Veneno para mi marido* (Poison for My Husband). No Madrid theatrical season since has been without a play by Alfonso Paso, and it has not been uncommon to find several works by this indefatigable writer on the boards at the same time. By 1971 his total output had exceeded 125 titles. Paso's name has come to be synonymous with popular, ephemeral comedy, but his writing has not been exclusively limited to humorous, suspenseful, or totally evasive theater. Such serious efforts as *Los pobrecitos* (The Poor, Sad People, 1957), *No hay novedad, Doña Adela* (Nothing New, Doña Adela, 1959), and the experimental *Nerón-Paso* (Nero-Paso, 1969) testify to his versatility and capacity for creating dramatic works that are more than routine.

III *The Contributions of The Prewar Generation*

Without the special contributions of several writers who first entered the theatrical life of Madrid in the late 1920's and early 1930's and who resumed their careers in the postwar period, the contemporary theater of Spain would have been far less colorful and, indeed, the degree of improvement in staging, acting, and dramatic quality in general would have been impossible. Although Buero and Sastre have been instrumental in creating an innovative drama of social consequence, other playwrights—some years older than either—have contributed works of substantial dramatic interest, in some instances ensuring an adequate staging of their plays by serving effectively in the additional capacity of director. Outstanding in artistry among this senior group of dramatists are José López Rubio (b. 1903)—prominent as a director, as an adapter of many important foreign works for the Spanish stage, and as the author of some eighteen original plays—and Miguel Mihura (b. 1905), considered by many to be the finest Spanish humorist of his time.

López Rubio entered the Madrid literary world at an early age; and in 1929 *De la noche a la mañana* (Overnight), a drama he had written in collaboration with Eduardo Ugarte Pagés, received the first prize in a contest for new playwrights sponsored by the newspaper *A B C*. The following year he accepted a contract with Metro-Goldwyn-Mayer to prepare Spanish versions of films produced in Hollywood. In 1949 he rejoined the ranks of Spanish dramatists with *Alberto*, a well-conceived play about the effects of uncontrolled illusion on the lives of a group who live a protected existence in a Madrid pension. The premiere of *Alberto* contributed additional significance to the year that also saw the production of Buero's *Story of a Stairway*, but it was *Celos del aire*[7] in 1950 that won for López Rubio almost unanimous critical admiration and the Fastenrath Prize for drama from the Royal Spanish Academy. Although his greatest popularity resulted from a series of serious comedies (several of them noticeably Pirandellian in manner) which were alternately satiric and poetic, two of his most impressive efforts are *Las manos son inocentes* (Our Hands are Innocent, 1958), a stark and uncompromising study of moral decay, and the unproduced *La puerta del ángel* (The Way of the Angel), a somber and violent drama set in provincial Spain.

Both López Rubio and Mihura have sometimes been accused of being purveyors of a *teatro de evasión* ("theater of evasion"), a facile critical tag which represents a narrow understanding of two writers whose works reveal only occasional similarities in spite of a mutually shared debt to Jardiel Poncela, a close associate of their early years. Like López Rubio, Mihura wrote his first plays with various collaborators. In 1952 he launched an independent career with the production of *Tres sombreros de copa* (Three Top Hats), a remarkable play which he had written some two decades earlier and which represented a unique intertwining of the farcical and the pathetic. The admiration that Eugène Ionesco has expressed for *Three Top Hats* has been frequently noted,[8] and the play has achieved the status of a classic of the modern Spanish theater.

Mihura's subsequent works have ranged from absurdist mysteries—such as *Carlota* (1957), *Melocotón en almíbar* (Peaches and Syrup, 1958) and *La tetera* (The Teapot, 1965) in which the mystery genre itself is satirized at times—to plays of the type of *Sublime decisión* (Sublime Decision, 1955) and *La bella Dorotea* (The Fair Dorothea, 1963), which are closer in spirit and impact to *Three Top Hats*.

A third dramatist to resume his career after a period devoted to other activities was Edgar Neville (1899-1968). Sometime novelist and successful film director, he wrote for the stage far less frequently than either López Rubio or Mihura. Nevertheless, when he returned to playwriting in 1952, his first new work, *El baile* (The Dance), became one of the major popular successes of the contemporary Spanish theater and exerted its charm over critics as well as the general public. An unabashedly sentimental but undeniably appealing play, *The Dance* served as a splendid vehicle for the talents of the actress Conchita Montes. *Adelita* (1954), the sequel to *The Dance*, proved far less effective dramatically, but Neville went on to demonstrate his refined sense of comic dialogue and techniques in several popular works that followed.

The other prominent figures of the prewar generation—José María Pemán (b. 1898), Joaquín Calvo-Sotelo (b. 1905), and Juan Ignacio Luca de Tena (b. 1897)—have produced works that cover a wide spectrum of traditional theater, including historical drama, reworkings of classical themes, mysteries, dramas of conscience, domestic comedies, and farce. Pemán's career has continued virtually uninterrupted since 1928. During the years of the

Spanish Republic, he wrote a series of historical plays in verse, following the example of the early twentieth-century poet-dramatist Eduardo Marquina. In the contemporary period he has enjoyed an enduring popularity with a segment of the theater public. Although not an active supporter of the Franco regime, Pemán's oft-acknowledged monarchist sympathies and his staunch Catholicism have earned him equally enduring political grace. On several occasions he has been suggested by the press as a suitable choice for the Nobel Prize for Literature, though there is no evidence that he has been seriously considered in Sweden. Pemán's efforts in the postwar period include *Electra* (1949), a treatment of the Greek theme in modern Spanish somewhat in the manner of Giraudoux; adaptations of several works of classical theater; prose dramas such as *Callados como los muertos* (Silent as the Dead, 1952), *En las manos del hijo* (In the Hands of the Son, 1953), and the more recent *Tres testigos* (Three Witnesses, 1970); he also wrote the farcical *Las tres etcéteras de Don Simón* (Don Simon's Three Etceteras, 1958). He is one of the more prolific of Spanish dramatists and continues, in spite of his age, to be active in the theatrical life of Madrid.

Like Pemán, Calvo-Sotelo is a remarkably productive writer, and his some fifty pieces for the stage reveal considerable variety in thematic material as well as occasional experiments with unconventional form. Brother of the assassinated leader of the conservative ranks in the republican government, Calvo-Sotelo has created a body of theatrical works that tend to favor traditional family and religious values. His most widely discussed play, which marks the high point of his career, is the drama of conscience *La muralla* (The Wall, 1954). In addition to many other serious plays such as *La ciudad sin Dios* (The Godless City, 1972), *El proceso del Arzobispo Carranza* (The Trial of Archbishop Carranza, 1964) and *El poder* (Power, 1965), he has written a number of comedies, none of which rises to the level of the best comic invention of the period. Light works of the caliber of *Una muchacha de Valladolid* (A Girl from Vallodolid, 1957) and its sequel, *Cartas credenciales* (Credentials of a Diplomat, 1960), epitomize the escapist theater deplored by many critics and by no means represent the strongest qualities of Calvo-Sotelo as a dramatic writer.

Juan Ignacio Luca de Tena (The Marquis of Luca de Tena) is

the past director of the major Madrid daily *A B C* and of the long established weekly magazine *Blanco y Negro* and is a man of strong royalist sympathies. Although he has written more than forty works for the stage, his production since 1949 seems relatively modest when compared with that of Calvo-Sotelo or Pemán. The plays which represent him best in the last two decades are the two sentimental historical dramas based on the ill-fated reign of Alfonso XII—*¿Dónde vas, Alfonso XII?* (Where Now, Alfonso XII?, 1957) and *¿Dónde vas, triste de ti?* (Where Now, Sad Friend?, 1959)—and his neo-Pirandellian success *¿Quién soy yo?* (*Who am I?*, written in 1935 and revived in 1968), which was followed by the play which supplied the answer, *Yo soy Brandel* (I am Brandel, 1969).

A special case among the prewar dramatists is that of Alejandro Casona (pseudonym of Alejandro Rodríguez Alvarez, 1903-1965) who spent the prime years of his career outside of Spain. Winner of the Lope de Vega Prize for Drama in 1933 for his *La sirena varada* (*The Stranded Mermaid*), Casona had elected to leave Spain at the outbreak of the civil war to take up residence in Mexico. Later he moved on to Buenos Aires where his major plays—*La dama del alba* (The Lady of the Dawn, 1944), *La barca sin pescador* (The Boat without a Fisherman, 1945), *Los árboles mueren de pie* (Trees Die Standing, 1949), and *La tercera palabra* (The Third Word, 1953)—were first performed.

The fantastic or the supernatural are integral parts of much of Casona's work, while the social and the political figure only peripherally. With the exception of *Nuestra Natacha* (Our Natacha, 1936), a deeply felt plea for educational reform in Spain, his theater has scant ideological substance, and today even this work seems to us an unlikely subject for controversy. Nevertheless, because of his republican sympathies Casona's exile lasted twenty-five years. Urged by friends who were still active in the theater in Spain, he returned to his homeland in 1962 for the Madrid premiere of *The Lady of the Dawn*. His reception was warm and sentimental; and the following year he returned permanently to see a number of the plays he had written over a period of two decades welcomed by an adoring public and a respectful but less enthusiastic corps of critics. Unfortunately, he was unable to resume his career with vigor. Weakened by a heart condition, he underwent surgery in the summer of 1965 and died a few months later. He produced only one new original drama, *El caballero de las espuelas de oro* (The Gentleman with the Golden Spurs, 1965), an historical play based on episodes in the life of the Golden Age writer Quevedo which was at least partly inspired by Buero-Vallejo's turn to historical themes between 1958 and 1963.[9]

Other writers of the prewar generation whose names figure in the Spanish theater since 1949 but with less impact are Claudio de la Torre (b. 1897), Horacio Ruiz de la Fuente (b. 1905), José Antonio Giménez Arnau (b. 1903), Max Aub (1902-1972),[10] Julia Maura (1910-1971) and the humorist Tono (Antonio de Lara) (b. 1898), who collaborated with Mihura before 1949 and was associated with him in the operation of the unique humor review *La Codorniz.*

IV *The Second Group of Postwar Dramatists*

Between 1955 and 1965 a second, larger group of post-civil war playwrights began to figure prominently in the contemporary theater of Spain. That a number of their plays—often harsh and realistic in tone—were produced and found a degree of public acceptance indicates that theatrical perspectives had become somewhat broader even in the commercial arena. This was due no doubt in part to the early efforts of Buero and Sastre as well as to Spain's renewed contacts with the world community.

Carlos Muñiz (b. 1927), José María Rodríquez Méndez (b. 1925), Ricardo Rodríguez Buded (born in the 1920's; the exact date is not known), Lauro Olmo (b. 1923), and José Martín Recuerda (b. 1925) have been described as the outstanding exponents of a new *teatro de protesta y denuncia* ("theater of protest and indictment"),[11] a label that serves only in a general way to identify their role as writers of serious drama which treats—at times with boldness—some of the more painful actualities of Spanish social and economic life. Rodríguez Buded's *Un hombre duerme* (A Man is Sleeping, 1959), Muñiz's *El tintero* (The Inkwell, 1960), and Olmo's *La camisa* (The Shirt, 1961) and *English Spoken (1968)* are representative examples of the Spanish theater of social criticism which concentrates on the problems of the poor and working classes and attempts to bring into sharp focus the defects of Spanish society as it presently exists.

José Martín Recuerda was the first Lope de Vega Prize recipient since Buero-Vallejo to establish himself firmly with subsequent works of quality. In the award-winning *El teatrito de Don Ramón* (Don Ramón's Small Theater, 1958), *Las salvajes en Puente San Gil* (The Savages in Puente San Gil, 1963), and *Como las secas cañas del camino* (Like the Dry Stalks Along the Way, 1965) he has cultivated a type of drama that cannot be considered realistic in the strictest interpretation of the term. Martín Recuerda's plays reveal strong lyrical and poetic overtones, with touches of the grotesque and the sensuous; and, on occasion, pure theatrical effect applied skillfully, with full awareness of the visual possibilities of dramatic art.

A somewhat younger playwright, Antonio Gala (b. 1936), won the Calderón de la Barca National Prize for Theater and attracted unusual critical praise in 1963 with *Los verdes campos del Edén* (The Green Fields of Eden), a moving drama dealing with the plight of a group of dispossessed people who take refuge in a cemetery crypt. In the eyes of some observers of Madrid's theater, the warm endorsement which the veteran dramatist Alejandro Casona gave to Gala's first play did little to enhance the youthful writer's reputation.[12] But the several works that have followed—*El sol en el hormiguero* (The Sun on the Ant Hill, 1965), *Noviembre y un poco de yerba* (November and a Bit of Grass, 1967), and *Los buenos días perdidos* (The Good Days Lost, 1972)—show Gala to be a writer of originality whose talent—potentially perhaps the finest of his generation—speaks for itself.

Only two members of the newer group of postwar dramatists have enjoyed an extended commercial success. Both Jaime Salom (b. 1925) and Juan José Alonso Millán (b. 1936) have joined the ranks of the most frequently performed Spanish playwrights. Salom won his first dramatic award in 1948 for a work written during his student days, but his entry into the professional theater dates from 1955, when *El Mensaje* (The Message) was performed in Bilbao. His early career was centered in Barcelona, but in the 1960's he became closely associated with the Madrid stage. Adopting the formula of several of the older generation of Spanish dramatists for success and professional longevity (if not for establishing a firm literary reputation), Salom has varied his production, creating such disparate plays as his violent and melodramatic drama of the civil war, *La casa de las chivas* (The House of the "Chivas", 1969), the metaphysical *La playa vacia* (The Empty Beach, 1969), and the contrived satirical comedy *Parchis Party* (Parchesi Party, 1965).

Alonso Millán, like Antonio Gala, is approximately a decade younger than most of the group of postwar dramatists who followed Buero and Sastre, and he belongs to the generation that grew up with little or no memory of the civil war years in Spain. Until recently he made no pretense of being more than a creator of entertainment for a public that wants to be amused for two hours before or after dinner. Since 1969 he has made an occasional venture into a more serious type of theater which combines suspense and a moral dilemma—most effectively to date in *Juegos de sociedad* (Society Games, 1970), a drama whose title suggests a frivolous play rather than a genuinely disturbing work concerning an indifference to moral responsibility masked by frivolity. Alonso Millán's plays are spiced with the most contemporary Americanisms of present-day Spanish speech, and they document certain changes in peninsular thought and expression that the purist might prefer to overlook.

In terms of national origin and age, Fernando Arrabal (b. 1932) could be considered a member of the postwar generation of Spanish dramatists, but his work actually figures only marginally in the contemporary theater of Spain.[13] After completing law studies at the University of Madrid, Arrabal took up residence in France in 1954 and, like the Irish Beckett and the Rumanian Ionesco, he now writes in French. Nevertheless, it must be recognized that the major influences on Arrabal have been Spanish in spite of his prolonged contact with the absurdist theater in France. He himself has admitted that when he wrote his first plays he had never heard of Beckett, Adamov, Ionesco, or Jarry (writers whose influence on Arrabal has been suggested).[14] On March 1, 1962, he commented in a letter to José Monleón: "In all my work I believe that it would be easiest to find the influences of Góngora (father of sordidness and ambiguity), Cervantes (master of the Cabala), Goya . . . and Gómez de la Serna . . . , and if you must seek a foreigner, I would have to name Lewis Carroll."[15]

One should not assume that a veil of secrecy surrounds the person and work of Arrabal in his homeland. Although his boldest and most scatological plays—which have inspired admiration, indignation, and censorial prohibitions in several countries—could not expect to achieve authorized production in Madrid at this time, a number of his works have been seen on the Spanish stage. *El triciclo* (The Tricycle) was premiered in 1958 before an audience that showed noisy disapproval[16] and appeared in printed form in 1966; the Spanish version of *Ceremony for a Murdered Black* was performed in 1965 and published the following year in *Primer Acto*, along with articles on Arrabal's theater; the publication of *Fando y Lis* (Fando and Lis) in 1967 followed a production in Barcelona. *El cementerio de automóviles* (Automobile Graveyard), *Ciugrena* (Guernica), and *Los dos verdugos* (The Two Executioners) have been available since 1965 in an edition which includes the playwright's essay on the theater of panic and selections from his correspondence with José Monleón. (However, in 1970 a production of *The Two Executioners* was suppressed by order of the censors.) Arrabal's much publicized contretemps with the authorities during a visit to Spain in 1967 and his twenty-five days of imprisonment led him to write *And They Put Handcuffs on the Flowers*, the work which has brought him most recognition (and notoriety) in the United States.[17]

V *Developments in the Spanish Theater Since 1965*

In recent years the Spanish theater has lost the veteran writers Alejandro Casona (d. 1965), Edgar Neville (d. 1968), Carlos Llopis (d. 1970), and Julia Maura (d. 1971), while the list of new playwrights to appear on the scene has grown longer. Despite the large number of entries, the Lope de Vega Prize was not awarded in 1965, 1966, and 1967; but productions of the winning plays from other years—*Epitafio para un soñador* (Epitaph for a Dreamer) by Adolfo Prego (1963);[18] *Te espero ayer* (I'll Wait for You Yesterday) by Manuel Pombo Angulo (1968); *Los niños* (The Offspring), by Diego Salvador (1969); and *Proceso de un régimen* (Trial of a Régime) by Luis Emilio Calvo Sotelo (1970)—indicated that the energies of talented newcomers were being directed toward the creation of varied forms of drama. Ana (Isabel) Diosdado, daughter of the acclaimed dramatic actress Amelia de la Torre and the first woman dramatist among the youngest group of writers, attracted favorable attention with *Oliva los tambores* (*Forget the Drums*, for which she was awarded the Mayte Prize for Theater in 1971), and *Okapi* (1972).

Several of the plays of Jorge Díaz, a young Chilean already recognized as a leader among the vanguard playwrights of South America, have been seen in Madrid since Díaz became a resident of Spain in 1965. Pedro Laín Entralgo, a member of the prewar generation best known as an academician and essayist, produced the timely *Cuando se espera* (When We Wait) in 1967, providing evidence that imaginative theatrical writing was not the province solely of younger dramatists. One of the most promising of the new playwrights is Juan Antonio Castro (born in 1927 and thus a contemporary of Sastre, Martín Recuerda, Muñiz, and Rodríguez Méndez); his stirring *Tiempo de 98* (Times of 98, 1970), based on writings of the Generation of '98, and *Ejercicios en la noche* (Exercises in the Night, 1971) are accomplishments of genuine intellectual and dramatic quality.

José Ruibal (b. 1925), José María Bellido (b. 1922), and Antonio Martínez Ballesteros (b. 1929) are the leaders among the so-called underground playwrights of Spain.[19] Since 1965 these writers have been attracting interest, and productions of their plays are no longer limited to university and experimental groups. All three have dedicated their efforts for a number of years to a mode of theater which is generally brief, allegorical, and intensely ironical, and which represents a rejection of both the naturalism of the social realists of Spain and the pseudorealism of the drawing-room playwrights. Publication of several of the works of Ruibal, Martínez Ballesteros, and Bellido in English translations in the American review *Modern International Drama* and the appearance of representative examples of their writing in *Primer Acto* and in the "Colección Teatro" series have contributed to their growing recognition both in Spain and abroad. Ruibal has lectured at several North American universities, and his full-length play *El asno* (The Jackass)—a work which satirizes the materialism of the "Yankee" entrepreneur and his gullible victims—was produced in New York by the off-Broadway group *Nuestro Teatro* in 1972 under the personal supervision of the playwright.

The editors of *Primer Acto* have documented the work of Carlos Pérez Dann (b. 1936), Luis Matilla (b. 1939), and Angel

García Pintado (b. 1941), a younger group of underground playwrights whose production has been fairly extensive but who remain virtually unknown except within a small circle of cognoscenti who have access to their unpublished manuscripts.[20] Juan M. (Martínez) de la Vega (b. 1942), Vicente Romero Ramírez (b. 1947), and Manuel Martínez Medeiro (b. 1939), who have become known among university groups and have been performed in drama competitions, were represented in the anthology *Teatro difícil* (Difficult Theater) published in 1971.

With the opening of the several *cafés-teatro* ("café-theaters") in Madrid since the Lady Pepa presented its first production in 1969,[21] opportunities for the performance of unconventional and experimental plays by both new and established writers have increased. These small, cabaret-type houses bring audiences into close proximity with the performers and permit a type of theatrical experience that would be impossible to achieve in less intimate surroundings. However, it would be erroneous to suppose that the *cafés-teatro* are the focal point of a new and liberated Spanish drama. Some of the fare is little more than a reduction of the type of popular comedies seen in the larger theaters or consists of musical skits of no great bite or originality. At the same time, there have been effective satirical revues and more than a few productions of works by unconventional dramatists such as Ruibal, Gala, and Romero Ramírez—as well as an occasional atypical work from senior playwrights associated with the theatrical establishment.

VI *Foreign Plays on the Contemporary Spanish Stage*

Works by virtually all of the important non-Spanish contemporary world dramatists have been staged in Spain since 1949, either by professional companies or experimental groups, and most of the popular successes of New York, London, and Paris have quickly found their way to the theaters of Madrid or Barcelona. Beckett, Genet, Williams, Miller, Albee, Weiss, Dürrenmatt, and Anouilh are all names familiar to Spanish audiences, and a great many other playwrights could be included on the list. Classical works by Molière, Shakespeare, and the Greek dramatists have also been restaged as well as *comedias* by Lope de Vega, Calderón, and Tirso de Molina from Spain's own rich Golden Age heritage.

A high percentage of the translations of foreign plays has been made by the contemporary Spanish dramatists themselves. Buero-Vallejo has adapted *Hamlet* (for a production in which Adolfo Marsillach portrayed the Danish prince) and Brecht's *Mother Courage;* Sastre has been represented by a version of *Medea,* translations of Langston Hughes's *Mulatto,* O'Casey's *Red Roses for Me* and Weiss's *Marat-Sade;* the translation of Albee's *A Delicate Balance* was made by Antonio Gala, and that of Greene's *Complaisant Lover* by Pemán; and the drama critic Enrique Llovet provided the adaptation for the controversial Marsillach production of Molière's *Tartuffe* in which the present-day Spanish technocracy was boldly satirized.

Perhaps the most important playwright-translator has been José López Rubio, whose contributions over a period of more than two decades cover a spectrum of European and American theater from Molière's *The Miser* and *The Would-be Gentleman* to Oscar Wilde's *The Importance of Being Earnest* and Arthur Miller's *Death of a Salesman* (a work that has been especially admired in Spain since its Madrid première in 1952). López Rubio has also adapted the Rodgers and Hammerstein musicals *South Pacific* and *The Sound of Music* and provided a translation for *Man of La Mancha* which proved acceptable to Castilian-speaking audiences—though not overwhelmingly successful at the box office.

VII *Music and Lyric Theater in Spain*

Musical theater represents a somewhat smaller part of theatrical fare in Spain than in the United States. The great age of the *zarzuela* had passed even before the establishment of the Second Republic in 1931; however, in the postwar period new productions of the classics of the *zarzuela* repertory continue, and this lyric genre peculiar to Spain remains popular both in live performances and on television. Spanish adaptations of *South Pacific, Fiddler on the Roof, My Fair Lady,* and several other American musicals have enjoyed a modest success in Madrid or Barcelona, and there have been musical versions of Spanish plays such as *La vida en un hilo* (based on Edgar Neville's popular comedy of that title) and *¡Ay, Angelina!* (based on Jardiel Poncela's *Angelina o el honor de un brigadier* and adapted by Alfonso Paso, son-in-law of the late playwright). Original Spanish musicals have been varied in content. López Rubio's *El caballero de Barajas* (with music by Manuel Parada)[22] was fashioned along the lines of the American musical, while the more recent *Castañuela 70* consisted of a series of independent sketches, representing a serious attempt at social and political satire. Contemporary Spanish opera is virtually nonexistent;[23] the Liceo Opera House in Barcelona offers the most important productions of standard operatic works to be seen in Spain.[24]

VIII *Aspects of Theatrical Production in Spain*

In 1970 there were some thirty theaters in Madrid alone utilized exclusively for live theatrical entertainment.[25] Four of these receive government support through the Ministry of Information and Tourism: The María Guerrero, presently under the supervision of José Luis Alonso; the Español, directed by Miguel Narros; the Teatro Nacional de Cámara, used for experimental works and new plays whose audience potential is considered to be limited; and the Teatro de la Zarzuela, where old works of the *zarzuela* genre are restaged and large scale productions of musical comedies and opera are also presented. Barcelona has a smaller number of theaters; only one, the Calderón de la Barca, enjoys the status of "national theater."[26]

A peculiarity of stage functions in Spain is the custom of two daily performances—a "matinee" at 7 P.M. and an evening performance at 10:30 or 11:00 (frequently seven days a week). The price of a theater ticket is still low in spite of a rise of fifty percent since 1960 and a hundred percent since 1950, and impresarios argue that two performances a day are an economic necessity. The system limits the running time of a play to approximately two hours and also places extraordinary physical demands on the performers. Buero-Vallejo, a leader in the protest against the double performance custom, has refused to write his plays to conform to the time limitations, and although cuts must be made to shorten his dramas on occasion, these cuts are always printed and indicated in the published texts of his works. Although lacking an effective organization for protest, some four hundred actors joined forces in 1972, and discussions were initiated with management to reform the system and to limit an actor's work to six days.

Given the vast amount of theatrical activity in Spain, a wide variance in production standards can be expected. Because of economic exigencies (or sometimes simply caution), a good play with skilled actors may be presented to the public in unimaginative or even shabby settings. However, on occasion a high degree of artistic and technical proficiency has produced such notable stage settings as the adaptable trampoline for the Víctor García production of *Yerma* and the simpler but eminently effective basic set for Juan Antonio Castro's *Times of 98.*

The roster of Spanish directors and performers contains a wide array of fine talent. Among the more notable names are the directors José Osuna, Emilio Burgos, Cayetano Luca de Tena, José Luis Alonso, and Víctor García; actor-directors Enrique Diosdado and the more youthful Adolfo Marsillach;[27] playwright-directors Miguel Mihura, Víctor Ruiz Iriarte, and José López Rubio; actresses Amelia de la Torre, Tina Gascó (dedicatee of plays by Buero, López Rubio, and Ruiz Iriarte), Conchita Montes (Madrid's leading exponent of high comedy roles), Victoria Rodríguez (wife of Buero-Vallejo), and Nuria Espert; actors Guillermo Marín and Carlos Lemos (both famous for portrayals of roles in classical drama), Enrique Diosdado, and Fernando Rey (known internationally as a motion picture actor). There are also numerous character actors and actresses who are held in esteem by the public as well as a younger generation of promising performers.

IX *Censorship and the Contemporary Spanish Theater*

All new dramatic works for the Spanish stage have been subject to some form of censorship since the end of the Civil War in 1939. The nature of the restrictions has generally been unclear to outside observers, and only one Hispanist from the United States (Patricia W. O'Connor) has attempted a serious study of the institution and its effects on creativity.[28] Until 1963 the readers of manuscripts were designated by the Ministry of Information and Tourism. Since these readers were frequently priests—with no precise norms to guide them—approval or rejection, determined by what the readers considered beneficial or harmful to the state or the Church, could be quite unpredictable. Works denied performance one year were sometimes granted approval at another time with insignificant changes, and plays were often approved for publication when public performance was prohibited. A good illustration is Buero-Vallejo's *Adventure in Grayness*, a controversial drama of political slant which was approved many years after its original submission and performed in a version that was somewhat stronger than the original one.[29]

In 1963 censorship was relaxed to a degree. Official norms were established, and a regular censorship committee, mostly lay, was appointed. The basic restrictions prohibit any situation or dialogue that would give offense to the Catholic Church or the person of the Chief of State, or that would threaten the security of the State. A casual comparison of plays published since 1963 with earlier works reveals blunter dialogue and bolder treatment of sexual themes and political matters in the writings of the past decade, even though a long list of moral taboos still exists. While the press was excluded from precensorship in 1966 and granted a kind of self-regulatory status over publications (which are subject to confiscation and fines), the performing arts still require prior authorization.[30]

When asked in a recent interview if his plays would have been better or different if there had not been censorship in Spain, Buero-Vallejo remarked: "Different, but I don't believe [they'd be] a great deal different. Different phrasings and details; perhaps two or three other works written and performed. But I think that I would have also written the ones that I have written. I've tried to follow my own way, with or without censorship. Without it I would have worked, to be sure, more and better."[31] In a similar interview, Juan José Alonso Millán, a younger writer whose plays have enjoyed exceptional popularity in the past decade, described censorship as an institution that has outlived the reasons for its original imposition and admitted that in his own writing he had consciously avoided controversial themes that would exclude a play from possible production.[32]

Probably no Spanish writer has been hampered more than Alfonso Sastre by censorship. This is due in part to this dramatist's persistent attacks on the institution of censorship itself, with resultant backlash against all of his works, even plays that can hardly be construed as openly critical of the Spanish government. It is easy to imagine that certain plays by other contemporary writers which have been produced successfully in

Madrid would have been proscribed had they come from the pen of Sastre. In Spain, as elsewhere, censorship has been at times erratic, inconsistent, and even vindictive.

Although governmental censorship of theater exists in many countries, including the modern nation of Israel, the restrictions imposed in Spain have inspired a more emotional condemnation in the United States than harsher restrictions which prevail in certain other nations, probably because of lingering political sympathies associated with Spain's civil war. There is no question but that an enduring anti-Spanish mood has been an obstacle to the wide acceptance of contemporary dramatic writing from Spain. While one must deplore the shackling effects of censorship on any form of artistic creativity, it is questionable that censorship alone can prevent the development of a major dramatic talent. In a report on the World Theater Season in London in 1972, Charles Marowitz remarked: "One of the fictions dearest to the radical temperament is that repressive, right-wing governments discourage the production of first class art. If theaters in Russia, East Berlin, and Czechoslovakia hadn't already demolished that myth, the present World Theater Season at the Aldwych certainly would, for among the companies garnered . . . as the finest in the world are representatives from South Africa, Spain, Greece, and Poland—which tends to suggest that whatever the political complexion of a society, it is no bar to artistic output—even if, as is the case in some of these countries, the artist has to risk his life to be heard."[33] Although there are many indications that censorship has indeed frustrated and inhibited artistic expression in Spain, there is also undeniable evidence in the body of work of more than one living Spanish playwright of bold and original writing for the stage.

CHAPTER 2

Leading Dramatists of the Prewar Generation

1 *José López Rubio*

J OSÉ López Rubio was born on December 13, 1903, in the small Mediterranean city of Motril in southern Spain, but he has lived the major part of his life in a more cosmopolitan environment, in close contact with the world of literature, theater, and film. His early dramatic efforts were all undertaken in collaboration with other young aspiring playwrights. Two plays attempted with Jardiel Poncela were never performed;[1] one of the two comedies written with Edgar Neville was adapted by the successful dramatist Honario Maura and produced in 1928 without mention of the real authors.[2] In 1929 López Rubio and Eduardo Ugarte Pagés were the winners of a contest for new writers sponsored by the Madrid daily *A B C*, and the production of their play *De la noche a la mañana* (Overnight) was highly successful.[3] López Rubio completed two other dramas with Ugarte (only one of which was performed) before leaving Spain for the United States, where he spent a number of years producing dialogue for Spanish versions of American films. Although busily engaged in cinematic work, the young writer did not lose interest in his career as a dramatist. In 1935 he began work on *Celos del aire* (Jealous of the Air) the play that was to establish him as an important playwright in Madrid some fifteen years later.

After the civil war, López Rubio returned to Spain and was engaged in scriptwriting and directing until 1947. The premiere of *Alberto,* on April 29, 1949, was a significant turning point for him, for it was on that occasion that an independently written play of his was first presented to the public. Earlier, the playwright had read both *Alberto* and *Una madeja de lana azul celeste* (A Skein of Sky-Blue Wool) to the director Luis Escobar, who selected the former for production in the María Guerrero Theater. López Rubio has noted that "*Madeja* is an easy comedy, while *Alberto* is a difficult work. Luis Escobar preferred the difficult one."[4]

As the critic Torrente Ballester has pointed out,[5] *Alberto* is not a play without certain defects but it came as a clear affirmation of López Rubio's further potential as a dramatist. The production of the work occurred less than six months before the important premiere of Buero's *Story of a Stairway*, and although *Alberto* is an ironic comedy with poetic overtones and the Buero play a drama of tragic implication, the two plays do have more in common than merely having been first performed in the same year. Both have a single unifying dramatic element: the ever-present stairway in one and the nonexistent but influential Alberto in the other; both in their individual ways pose questions about the shortcomings of Spanish society; and both are open-ended plays that offer no unequivocal solutions and that demand serious reflection on the part of the audience.

The entire action of *Alberto* takes place in the comfortable *pensión*, where a varied group of individuals have found a haven from the annoying complexities of modern life. The first act is built around the ingenious resolution of a crisis brought on by the departure of the owner for South America. Without her guiding hand, the boarders will be forced to dissolve their present relationships and reestablish themselves. Leticia, a young stenographer with a tendency to be carried away by her own sense of the poetical, conceives a plan to invent a new "director" and provides him with the name "Alberto." The antithesis of Leticia is Doña Sofía, an utterly literal-minded woman who is accompanied by her overly sheltered daughter. The most forceful of the boarders is an old Marquesa who is attended by the browbeaten Doña Rosalía. The male contingent is composed of two older men: the talkative Don José, and Don Pascual, an employee in a government office. Javier, who is in love with Leticia, is a young dentist who frequents the establishment. All of the boarders are, in their individual ways, self-centered persons who practice the act of *evasión*, and it is this aspect of their natures that permits essentially practical-minded people to accept the idea of a nonexistent manager of their lives. Don José states the true reason for their seeking a retreat in the *pensión*:

DON JOSÉ. We are all here because we don't want responsibilities, because it is easy for us to pay and not think of the cost.[6]

The two older men discuss at some length the problems that Spaniards have in governing themselves and express a critical attitude toward their society, while the Marquesa delivers a pithy condemnation of "modern ways." To a degree, these and the other characters form a microcosm of Spanish bourgeois society, though this may be a by-product of the playwright's original intent.

In the second act of the play, it is apparent that each of the boarders has been endowing the mythical landlord with his or her own attitudes and desires. The physical appearance of the *pensión* has changed, for some of the furnishings have been replaced by pieces in better taste—Alberto's taste. It is in the liberation of their suppressed ambitions and emotions that the boarders are now revealing their inner natures. But for Javier, who lives outside the boundaries of the fantasy, Leticia's growing attachment to Alberto becomes disturbing. The young woman has fallen in love with her creation (Pygmalion and Galatea with a reversal of the sexes), and with a sense of urgency Javier attempts to explain to her that Alberto—if he existed—would possess the same weaknesses as other men. A new character identified as "The Other Woman" arrives in search of Alberto; and since she was not a member of the original "family," the implication is that Alberto has acquired an existence that enables him to act autonomously. In the third act, the boarders appear to have lost their sense of unity, for Alberto has gotten out of hand. "The Other Woman" calls again and now informs Leticia that Alberto has fled and is being sought by the police. Javier pretends to know the woman, but Doña Elena (who has returned disillusioned from America) recognizes the deception: she is really the young dentist's nurse playing a role. Although Javier's "play" had been devised to destroy Leticia's love for Alberto by portraying him as weak and capable of deceit, the cure has a stunning effect on the girl. The play ends on a note of uncertainty, for Leticia has not completely awakened from her dream; and when Javier asks her if he has done wrong, she can only answer: "I don't know, Javier. . .I don't know."[7]

Alberto is theater-within-theater, and only in approaching the work as a form of play-within-a-play can it be properly judged. The characters—each a "dramatist" in his own right—elect to perform a play in which the protagonist is imaginary. In order to achieve a sense of reality within the fantasy, each must contribute to the composition. Actually, the first act is a kind of prologue, for the play of "Alberto" cannot begin until the protagonist is invented and has an opportunity to assume a role (albeit unseen) in the second act. Javier decides to create a new play called "Alberto" which will be so astounding that it will discredit the version of Leticia. At the end of López Rubio's *Alberto*, the subplays have been interrupted without having reached a satisfactory conclusion, but there is an element of hope in the possibility that Javier and Leticia may find a common vision of reality.

The second play of López Rubio's new career was *Jealous of the Air*, the comedy begun in 1935 and reworked over a period of years. Both in Madrid and Barcelona the work was favorably received, and it won for its author the Fastenrath Prize for Drama of the Royal Spanish Academy. The quality of *Jealous of the Air* that was most admired at the time of the premiere was the polished dialogue, but Torrente Ballester, who had been critical of *Alberto*, also expressed warm praise for the dramatic skills displayed in the contrapuntal design of the play.[8] The work does indeed represent a masterful balancing of elements and a subtle movement between make-believe and reality. All of the characters are highly theatrical in concept and in behavior, and they are fully aware that they are performing life on a stage.

The setting of the play is a remote country estate in the Pyrenees. Because of financial difficulties the elderly owners, Don Pedro and Doña Aurelia, have rented part of their home to Bernardo and Cristina, a young couple from Madrid. However, there is no direct communication between them, for they have agreed on a kind of pretense which divides the house into two worlds. Neither couple speaks to the other, and an old servant named Gervasio serves as an intermediary, recognizing both couples when it is expedient. At first the eccentric behavior of the old people appears to be little more than a whimsical conceit of the playwright (Theodore Beardsley has included them among his examples of illogical characters in contemporary Spanish drama);[9] however, Don Pedro and his wife do have essential functions in López Rubio's dramatic design. Not only do they serve as commentators on the action but they also become an actual audience for a dual intrigue when the first couple is joined by a second (Enrique and Isabel) for a weekend in the country. And in the final scene they play an active role in the reconciliation of Bernardo and Cristina.

Cristina is uncontrollably jealous, and even when she has her husband completely isolated from temptation she continues to seek grounds for her suspicions. Enrique, who is a playwright by profession, suggests to Bernardo a cure:

ENRIQUE: Deceive her. It's preferable to face once and for all the danger that one fears rather than fear it forever. . .
BERNARDO: Shakespeare could have written that.
ENRIQUE: He did. I borrowed it from him. Cure her of her sickness . . . with the truth. Put the evidence in front of her. Either she's cured or she perishes. But she'll be cured, don't worry. No one has ever died of jealousy.[10]

Enrique proposes that Bernardo pretend to deceive Cristina with Isabel, an actress with a penchant for living every part she undertakes. Actually it will be unnecessary for Bernardo to pretend, for he and Isabel have already been having an affair which Enrique has not suspected. The moment the two are left alone they embrace passionately, providing a surprising and ironical ending for the first act. The succeeding action takes place the following day. Doña Aurelia and Don Pedro sit in their armchairs at one side of the stage as observers. Isabel analyzes her egotistical husband for Bernardo, explaining that as a lover Enrique had played a role which became boring after he had satisfied his basic desire. Until she met Bernardo, Isabel had resigned herself to the farce, "to draw cards in that game that is life for him. . . ."[11] It is not by mere chance that López Rubio has put the word *farsa* in Isabel's dialogue at this point, for he is clearly underlining the complete theatricalness of his characters' lives.

When Enrique has an opportunity to be alone with Cristina, he succeeds in arousing her suspicions by suggesting that Isabel is capable of using her charms on Bernardo—but he also begins to have doubts about the wisdom of his own plot. Finally he explains to Cristina that a plan had been devised to make her think that she had been deceived, and she in turn proposes that the playwright enact with her the same kind of deception in the presence of Isabel and Bernardo. When Bernardo's voice is heard from the garden, Cristina moves quickly. She curls up on the sofa next to Enrique and orders him to talk to her amorously. He is at a loss for lines, and Cristina becomes the playwright and suggests that he recite the names of the provinces of Spain. This final scene of the second act of *Jealous of the Air* is a delightful blend of nonsense and calculation. However, it has been suggested that López Rubio may have borrowed the basic idea. Marquerie relates it to a scene in Jardiel Poncela's *Es peligroso asomarse al exterior,* in which a telephone directory is read in an amorous manner.[12] Be that as it may, this remains one of the most appealing scenes of high comedy in contemporary Spanish dramatic literature.

At the opening of the final act, Don Pedro is indisposed but eventually comes downstairs to take his customary place with his wife in their *butacas* ("theater seats") to provide the audience for the intrigue that is being "performed" by the younger characters. Rather than representing a fantastic element in the play, they have now become the point of reference for basic reality. Isabel suspects that the interest between Cristina and Enrique is only a game; she also understands that Bernardo's growing jealousy reveals his real love for his wife and that her own affair with him cannot endure. Deciding that it is time to bow out with Enrique, Isabel enjoys a moment of vengeance before her exit. Earlier Cristina had discovered her with Bernardo in the garden "performing" a love scene, and she is still not certain whether it was staged for her benefit or played in sincerity. Isabel now confirms that the lovemaking had been genuine. The remainder of the dialogue falls to Don Pedro and Doña Aurelia. They have also faced the problem of deception and doubt and their union has survived. By listening to a description of the crisis that had occurred years before, Cristina and Bernardo are able to relate the experience of the old couple to their own relationship and to realize their essential need for each other.

As with *Alberto*, López Rubio has employed a type of play-within-a-play technique—in this case to reveal the absence of realistic communication in two marital situations that become intricately and humorously involved. Ironically, the communication between the two couples is more artificial than that between them and the elderly pair who invented an illusion around their lives to hide the reality that financial need has forced upon them.

The four younger characters are not fully developed individuals in the psychological sense; and because we see only facets of their personalities they are not completely believable. However, this does not keep them from being effective creations for an intellectual study of human ambivalence and self-delusion in a work which is rich in irony and insights. While a surface similarity to Molnar's *The Play's the Thing* may be apparent, *Jealous of the Air* is by no means imitative. It is a superior play of its kind, with trenchant and skillfully measured dialogue and an element of humanity that is lacking in the Hungarian playwright's Pirandellian comedy.

In 1951, *A Skein of Sky-Blue Wool*, *Veinte y cuarenta* (Twenty and Forty), and *Cena de Navidad* (Christmas Dinner) were produced in rapid succession. Though these three works are not lacking in dramatic interest, none is of the quality of *Alberto* or *Jealous of the Air*; however, *Christmas Dinner* does offer pertinent insights into López Rubio's attempts to achieve variety in his dramatic efforts at this stage of his career. The "dinner" which gives the play its title takes place in a restaurant in an unnamed provincial city of Spain as the result of a newspaper advertisement which extends an invitation to any person who happens to be alone on Christmas Eve without friends or family. The use of some type of public accomodation—a restaurant, a bar, an ocean liner, or even a stagecoach—for bringing together a groups of diverse characters for dramatic or cinematic purposes is familiar. In the modern theater, playwrights of every bent from O'Neill and Genet to Williams and Wilson have utilized the device effectively. (It should be remembered that the action of *Alberto* is set in a *pensión*.) In *Christmas Dinner* the playwright has elected to work with a limited group of personages—perhaps fewer than the particular situation would seem to require. Undoubtedly the play is weakened because two of the characters who appear briefly in the first act as a result of the advertisement do not reappear in the drama (although it could be argued that they could have no meaningful function in the subsequent action). Only three persons actually share the dinner: Gabriel, who placed the newspaper notice; Laura, a young woman who turns out to be Gabriel's estranged wife; and Don Juan, an elderly cynic who has escaped from the stale family ritual at his home. And at the beginning of the second act, a fourth figure joins the group—a prostitute referred to as "The Bad Woman" (*la mala mujer*).

In order to present the story of Laura's discovery of her husband's infidelity and her separation from him, López Rubio devised a clever playlet-within-the-play (a not unexpected device in his work) in which Don Juan serves as director and Laura reenacts the events, with the prostitute performing the role of Julia, a friend and a confidante. Then, in an effective reversal of roles, Laura becomes Julia and the prostitute briefly assumes the part of Laura. Don Juan is a striking character who represents a tempting Devil with his cynical advice to Laura to indulge in life fully now that she is "free," and The Bad Woman is given her moment of grandeur when she cautions Laura against the philosophy of Don Juan, noting that "an open door may not be freedom at all—just the entrance to a bigger jail."[13]

Development of suspense and emotional tension are clearly more important in *Christmas Dinner* than in *Alberto* or *Celos del aire*, while there is a more pronounced moralistic tone than can be noted in any of López Rubio's previous works. But the play falls short of its theatrical possibilities, and it did not enjoy a notable public success. Nevertheless, Sainz de Robles considered the first act an example of the playwright's best work to date,[14] and López Rubio has expressed his personal satisfaction with other parts of this work.[15]

Between 1952, the year of the premiere of *El remedio en la memoria* (Remedy in Memory), and the fall of 1954, which saw the production of *La otra orilla* (The Other Shore), the career of López Rubio was in a period of artistic ascendency. Discounting the poorly received and unevenly written *Cuenta nueva* (A Clean Page), the other works produced during the two-year period rank among his best. Of the playwright's more important plays, *Remedy in Memory* has been, perhaps, the least appreciated. Although some of the reviews were quite favorable, the author himself expressed a degree of pique at the original reception of the play. "That work seemed too subtle and complicated. Hardly any of the critics recognized the double play of fiction and reality, of theater-within-theater. . . . It's curious; they ask you not to be superficial and when you aren't, they throw it up to you."[16] The theme of *Remedy in Memory* is the substitution of illusion for reality or, as Valbuena Prat expresses it, the "falsification of true reality. . .from living the life of the theater too deeply."[17] The protagonist of the drama, Gloria Velarde, is an actress whose private life is colored by the artificiality and illusion of her professional existence. Pirandello dealt with the effects of a theatrical career on the private life of an actress in *Trovarsi* (1932), and at the time of the premiere of *Remedy in Memory*, López Rubio conceded that the theme of his play was hardly new but added that his approach was original.[18]

From the opening scene, the character of Gloria Velarde dominates the action of the play—even though her actual entrance is postponed. The vanity of the woman and her unsatisfactory relationship with her daughter of eighteen (Luz María) are suggested through two purely visual actions. Virginia, a retired actress who has her attitudes firmly grounded in reality and who serves as a companion for Luz María, places photographs of Gloria in conspicuous spots around the sitting room of their summer house. The daughter enters and proceeds to remove them, for to her they are symbols of the career that has deprived her of genuine maternal love. Gerardo, a playwright and longtime associate of Gloria's in the theater, explains to Luz María the extent of her mother's involvement in acting:

GERARDO. There are two ways of being sincere—saying what is felt or feeling what is said, putting into it such passion . . . such sudden conviction, that for a moment it becomes true . . . . Theater is pretending, knowing that one is pretending, with intonation correct and posture calculated. The marvel of Gloria Velarde is that she has never gone on stage to act but to live other lives, to believe totally what she is saying, as if possessed. It may be that she lacks the talent to create for herself a character beforehand, that she is incapable of study and reflexion. But put her into the situation, supply the words for her, and the creative process begins.[19]

At the end of the first act, Gloria is faced with the startling news that her daughter is in love with Antonio, a man who is twice the girl's age and who had actually been the actress's own lover years before. She refuses to accept reality and swallows a bottle of sleeping pills (which prove to be only aspirin substituted by the watchful Virginia). To understand this play it must be remembered that this and subsequent actions of Gloria which smack of second-rate melodrama represent her attempts to deal with problems in terms of roles she has essayed on the stage.

Gloria tries to convince Antonio that he is too old for Luz María and delivers a speech worthy of the *efectista* theater of another age. She uses her talent well and is left perplexed when her former lover—quite aware of the meaninglessness of the words—exits calmly. Almost immediately she is required to assume the public role of "Gloria Velarde" by the appearance of Margarita, an aspiring young actress who has been seeking an interview. Gloria pretends to be interested in helping the girl and suggests that she learn a particular scene for an audition the following day. Before Margarita exits she is subjected to an exaggerated discourse on "the religion of the theater." Virginia discovers Gloria still caught up in the illusion of her "scene." She suggests that the actress go to bed, and Gloria answers her as if in a dream.

When Luz María appears and informs her mother that Antonio has told her the facts of the past and that her own love is unchanged, Gloria turns without hesitation to the theater for another card to play, implying in the dialogue that she has borrowed that Antonio is her daughter's real father. Margarita returns to perform the scene she has memorized, and Gloria instructs her to substitute "Antonio" for the original name "Luis" in the monologue. After Gloria's first "revelation," Luz María had spent the night away from home, but Gerardo has found her and has explained Gloria's purpose. The actress contrives to make Luz María believe that Antonio is the father of an illegitimate child; however, Margarita (in the role of the "mother") shows less talent than her mentor for making outmoded melodrama believable; she falters and forgets to substitute the name. The attempt to discredit Antonio fails, and Gerardo undertakes to explain to the actress the reasons for, and futility of, her aborted "performances." He expresses a note of hope for Gloria and the consolation that he, himself, has long loved her—though not so blindly as to risk marriage. The conclusion of *Remedy in Memory* is not a conventional "happy ending"; neither is it particularly disturbing, since the playwright does provide a light touch of humor through irony. Gloria Velarde is not a deeply tragic figure; but she remains a complex and interesting creation who is no doubt based in part on López Rubio's own experiences with performers during his long association with the theater.

La venda en los ojos (The Blindfold) was first performed on March 3, 1954, and received the National Prize for Theater for the season. It is an appealing, serious comedy which contains some of López Rubio's most accomplished dramatic writing, and it has shown its durability in a revival in 1963, under the new title *Extraño mundo de Beatriz* (The Strange World of Beatriz) and in a successful television production in 1972. In *The Blindfold*, López Rubio, like Jardiel Poncela, uses madness—or feigned madness—as the material of comedy,[20] but in subtle and unexpected ways he reminds us that just beneath the farce and in the extravagant inventions of the characters despair is also present. And in this play, more than in any of his other works, the playwright employs a type of absurdist dialogue similar to that which was exploited so extensively by Jardiel Poncela, with abrupt shifts of meaning and bizarre turns of thought in situations that are deliberately lacking in verisimilitude. However, the absurd and the unreal are skillfully blended with those elements that represent fundamental human experience so that the result is far from a dehumanization. The characters do not exist merely as an excuse for the dramatist's own verbal virtuosity.

In the opening scene, López Rubio plays with his audience, leading us to believe that knowledge of the illicit marital and commercial activities of a family described by one maid to another is essential to the appreciation of the action that is to ensue. But in reality what we have is a satire of a tired cliché of conventional exposition, for the characters discussed have no relationship whatsoever to the plot of the play and they are not mentioned again.

Beatriz, the protagonist of *The Blindfold*, stops time when her adored husband of one year abandons her, and she goes to the airport daily to meet Enrique, fully aware that he is not on the passenger list (though pretending to believe otherwise). Over a period of ten years she is abetted by her watchful aunt and uncle (Carolina and Gerardo). Their life has become a play in which Carolina assumes varied roles and for which Gerardo supplies an audience from the outside by advertising rare and unobtainable works of art to lure in a "Buyer." Beatriz herself engages in long telephone descriptions of her activities to a supposedly imaginary friend (Julia) who eventually proves to be quite real. The game is interrupted when Beatriz returns one day from the airport with a substitute Enrique in the person of an architect named Germán, who accepts the "role" and comes to love Beatriz.[21] When Julia produces the real Enrique—now sick and changed—Beatriz abandons her "insanity" long enough to admit her anguish and to reject him. At the end of the play, through an inspired manipulation of time, Beatriz erases Enrique from her life and indicates that she will seek a new life with Germán. It would be possible to interpret Beatriz's action as a definitive acceptance of madness, but a close reading of the dialogue suggests a somewhat different implication. For the first time, she now refers to the false Enrique by his real name, Germán; and although she speaks as if she had retreated into her adolescence, the retreat is just to a point in her life that she had reached before meeting the real Enrique. Whereas in *Remedy in Memory* López Rubio had treated the case of a woman who was unable to distinguish between illusion and reality, or, more specifically, theater and reality, and for whom illusion fails, he now presents consciously applied illusion as not being erroneous and as an acceptable solution to a predicament. Beatriz and her guardians structure their existence and cultivate the absurd as an antidote for the life that social convention could be expected to impose.

Only months after the premiere of *The Blindfold*, *La otra orilla* (The Other Shore) was produced and became one of the playwright's most popular and most frequently performed works. In his review for *Madrid*, the critic Gómez Picazo wrote: "The work is a meditation on the world from a place in which the passions of the world lose their value and hypocrisy gives way to truth. For this reason, it is not untranscendental, in spite of the humoristic wrapping . . . . It constitutes, on the contrary, a valid lesson on the fiction and blindness which seem to surround and to determine human actions and reactions."[22] *The Other Shore* offers some of López Rubio's most trenchant satire and effective irony, as well as the sobering implications that contemporary man is more often than not self-doomed to superficial liaisons in life and that the reasons for his failures may become clear only in the ultimate moment—if then.

In the opening scene of the play the four principals are killed, and although their ghosts remain visible to the audience, they cannot communicate with the other characters who remain alive. Ana and her lover Leonardo had been enjoying an illicit evening in the house of the latter's aunt. They are shot by Ana's "wronged" husband, Jaime, who is in turn killed by the police.

The fourth victim is Martín, who had been walking his dog in the street at an inopportune time and had happened to get in the way of Jaime's first shot. Death continues to be the great equalizer and also the eliminator of physical desires, but in the López Rubio work the dead people retain for a short time an interest in the world they are leaving. They remain temporarily at the scene of their demise and are able to observe the reactions of their relatives and associates. In the course of their own discussions, it is revealed that while each had been engaged in deception, each had also been the victim of some type of deceit.

Even in death López Rubio's creations are capable of lies and self-delusion. Ana maintains to Jaime that her meeting with Leonardo had been quite innocent—even though what Jaime had seen through the window had indicated otherwise—and that she had come to the house to reclaim some compromising letters for a friend named Eugenia. Ironically, Leonardo did have some letters from Eugenia and both Jaime and Martín had been involved with her at one time or another. The ghosts are amazed at the behavior of their survivors (Leonardo's wife, his sister-in-law, his wife's young lover, Martín's selfish nephew, and his lawyer) but they are helpless to protest (though the sister-in-law does sense their presence). The second act ends with the news—disclosed through a telephone call to a policeman, that one of the "dead" characters is really only in a coma. The audience is left in suspense because the policeman forgets to ask which one is still living; when he tries to call back, the line is busy. Through gradual elimination, as the spirits disappear through the French windows to begin their trip to the "other shore," it becomes evident which of the characters are really dead. First Jaime exits and then Leonardo. When they are left alone, Martín tells Ana that he loves her in spite of her defects. Ana, too, begins to disappear, and Martín calls after her. The telephone rings and the news arrives that the surviving victim has also died. The audience knows that it was Martín, who follows Ana, calling her name. Granted an initial acceptance of the supernatural element in *The Other Shore*, the couple's tardy discovery of their spiritual affinity is affecting; and only the most literal-minded could fail to respond to the theatrical impact of the final scene of the play when experienced in actual performance.

The Other Shore was followed in 1955 by the musical comedy

El caballero de Barajas (The Gentleman of Barajas), with book and lyrics by López Rubio and a score by Manuel Parada; and in 1956 by two new plays: *La novia del espacio* (The Love from Space), a poorly received work about a girl from La Mancha who becomes involved with a visitor from another planet, and *Un trono para Cristy* (A Throne for Cristy), a sentimental comedy about dispossessed royalty. Until the first performance of *Las manos son inocentes* (Our Hands are Innocent) on October 2, 1958, it might reasonably have been concluded that the dramatic talents of López Rubio would continue to find their most satisfactory expression in the area of intellectual comedy or poetic fantasy, and that deeply serious theater, unrelieved by humor or satire, would remain outside his realm of creative interest. However, the stark and uncompromising exploration of human guilt and remorse in *Our Hands are Innocent* revealed a new aspect of this playwright's vision. Buero-Vallejo himself saw fit to express his personal admiration for López Rubio's new venture when he wrote: ". . .the work is, for me, one of the best by its author and one of the most consummate of the season. But I am not referring merely to the example of his artistry but to that of his spiritual youth . . . May we all know—when we reach his present age—how to work in the same manner: to put ourselves once again on the threshold."[23] But the critical reception, while generally favorable, was qualified in several instances. Commenting on the warm reception accorded the play by the opening night audience, García Luengo observed; "As for the reaction of the public. . .it is probable that they felt moved by that drama or that, on the contrary, they were in the mood for a cold and cerebral dialectic game, like those to which the French are so addicted."[24] And after the Barcelona opening, Martí Farreras found the work less than convincing in spite of its "undeniable literary dignity."[25] But regardless of the differing opinions, *Our Hands are Innocent* is a solid and meritorious accomplishment.

The title is derived from a passage from Racine's neoclassic tragedy *Phèdre* (act 1, scene 3):

> Grâces au Ciel, mes mains ne sont point
> criminelles. . .
> Plût aux Dieux que mon coeur fût innocent
> comme elles!

The lines contain the essence of the playwright's theme and may also suggest that he has attempted a contemporary drama along classical lines. López Rubio calls *Our Hands are Innocent* a *duo coreado* ("duet with chorus"), which is as precise a description as could be desired, for the work is for the most part an extended dialogue or "debate" between the two principal characters, with choral commentary supplied by an elderly concierge.

The event around which the entire play centers takes place prior to the opening scene. It is the death of The Boarder (Señor Guevara) who had been living in a rented room in the shabby apartment of Germán and Paula, a middle-aged couple. Germán is an unsuccessful writer whose spirit has been eroded by continued failure to find recognition. His office job has only added to his frustration. Beset by pressing financial problems, the couple is tempted by the money that Guevara has in his possession and plots to kill him. The inner action of the two acts develops from a series of revelations concerning the actual cause of death. At first Germán and Paula believe that Guevara has died from two poison tablets which Paula had substituted for his customary medicine; but on examining the contents of a wastebasket, Paula discovers the tablets which she thought the Boarder had swallowed. Although they are not now technically murderers, the burden of guilt is not removed. A telephone call informs them that there is some question about the cause of Guevara's death and that an autopsy is to be performed. At this point they are faced with the ironic possibility that they may be accused of a crime of which they are innocent. The attorney of the dead man arrives, and a further irony is disclosed: the Boarder had praised the couple for their unselfishness and has left his money to them in a will. Since it is evident that he had overheard their discussion of their financial problems, it seems likely that he had also known of their plan to kill him. Suspicious of all human motives, Germán concludes that the will had only been part of a cruel design to let them go to the gallows with all their material needs satisfied. Then a police agent informs the couple that Guevara had left a suicide note indicating that no one should be blamed for his death; and when Paula discovers a tube of poison in the dead man's belongings, she realizes that he had at least contemplated suicide. However, the autopsy reveals that he had died of natural causes.

The symbolic use of light and darkness can be found throughout the drama, both in the dialogue and in the visual effects. At the end of the play, Paula tells her husband: "You must lead me by the hand. I am blind . . . and you are beginning to see."[26] Figuratively speaking, Paula is—like Oedipus—blind, and she looks to Germán, who has found the beginning of understanding (and light) to be her guide. After a final telephone call from the attorney relative to a later meeting with them (about the inheritance that Germán has decided to reject), the husband and wife prepare to leave the apartment. At Paula's request Germán extinguishes the last artificial light, for the brighter "cold light of day" is now beginning to illuminate the room.

Diana está comunicando (Diana's Mind is Busy, 1960) represented a return on the part of the playright to a lighter type of theater. The play is a brisk and entertaining farce which lacks the serious undertones of his most acclaimed work, but the leading role of a beautiful mental telepathist provided a splendid vehicle for the talents of the comedienne Conchita Montes. After the production of *Esta noche, tampoco* (Not Tonight Either, 1961), some three years elapsed before another new play by López Rubio was seen in Madrid. *Nunca es tarde* (It's Never Too Late, 1964) revealed a more introspective and less cynical writer. This story of an autumnal love that is shattered by death begins in a lighthearted manner—although in the dialogue of the protagonist (Flora) there are suggestions of the desperation of an aging woman who has enjoyed acclaim for her beauty and talent. In the second act, where the theatrical values are strongest, the mood shifts to the emotional and dramatic plane, and the act ends with a moving revelation of a fatal accident. The final act is curious, for we find Flora absorbed in her own illusions (considered as insanity by the daughter of her lost lover) only to be brought back to a belief in life by an abrupt and unexpected turn of events which she interprets to be evidence of a "sign" from the other world. The mingling of pathos and humor is characteristic of much of López Rubio's theater, but the preoccupation with the idea of time running out and with death gives *It's Never Too Late* a special flavor that sets the play apart from his other serious comedies.

From 1964 until 1971 no new play by López Rubio was performed. However, it was hardly a period of inactivity for the

multitalented writer. He adapted several American plays and
musicals, wrote film scripts, and worked on a projected history of
Spanish theater. He also completed a second serious drama, *La
puerta del ángel* (The Way of the Angel), which is yet to be
staged.[27] Set in a small town in the "ancient kingdom of León,"
the play deals with the return of a man (Julián) who had been
convicted fifteen years before of a murder he did not commit.
Both Norberta, who had actually murdered her husband because
of Julián, and Martirio, her companion, still desire him; and their
long years of waiting have not lessened their sexual impulses.
When it appears that Julián will find redemption with a young
woman (Aúrea) who loves him, Norberta causes the girl's death.
One is tempted to call this play López Rubio's *No Exit*, for at the
end Julián, Martirio, and Norberta are doomed to hate each other
in a hellish existence. Both *Our Hands are Innocent* and *The
Way of the Angel* are concerned with murder—plotted in one and
consummated in the other before the opening scenes. But while
the earlier work is coldly intellectual and devoid of sensuality,
The Way of the Angel is a drama in which sexual urges are ever
present and preordain the ultimate tragedy.

A series of brisk and dramatically varied television plays, called
Al filo de lo imposible (At the Edge of the Impossible) won for
López Rubio the National Television Award for the best dramatic
series in 1970. One of the short works, *Veneno activo* (Active
Poison) was adapted for the stage and produced at the
Café-Theater Stefanis in October, 1971. This macabre little black
comedy, with dialogue intentionally designed to sound like a too
literal translation into Spanish of a French play (resulting in an
unusual distortion of reality that complemented the action),
proved well suited for the intimate surroundings of the
café-teatro. Finally, the playwright returned in 1972 with a major
comedy, *El corazón en la mano* (With Heart and Soul), which
was awarded the National Prize for Theater for best play of the
season. Close in spirit to the works that had brought him most
recognition, *With Heart and Soul* was described by the critic
Adolfo Prego as a "captivating play of very personal
accent. . .which is, of course, among the three best that López
Rubio has written."[28]

In his serious comedies, López Rubio has achieved a style that
is recognizably his own through a skillful blending of irony and

satire with sentiment and poetic touches. His use of the Spanish language as a vehicle of dramatic expression has been impeccable (a virtue that critics have never failed to note), and his best plays are evidence of his taste, keen intellect, and sure sense of theatrical effect. The application of Pirandellian techniques in his works recalls at times the more persistent Pirandellian bent of Jean Anouilh in France; yet it should be remembered that the fascination for role-playing and the question of illusion versus reality are also part of a long Spanish tradition that stems from Cervantes and Calderón.

II *Miguel Mihura*

Miguel Mihura Santos (b. 1905) can justifiably be described as Spain's leading creator of humoristic theater of the last two decades. Yet the major phase of his career began only after many years of dividing his creative energies between screenwriting and occasional collaborative stage works and serving as director of the humor magazines *La Ametralladora* (from 1936 until 1939) and *La Codorniz* (which he founded in 1942). Son of the prominent actor-author and Madrid theatrical impresario Miguel Mihura Alvarez, the younger Mihura has literally lived in the world of theater from childhood. But his turn to playwriting does not seem to have been inevitable or perhaps even probable. His first work, *Tres sombreros de copa* (Three Top Hats) was written in 1932 during a period when he was confined to his home because of an operation on his leg. This unusual comedy was considered markedly avant-garde when Mihura first showed it to his associates in the theater, and its production was delayed at first by doubts about its appeal and later by the upheaval of the civil war. Although he went on to write a considerable amount of dialogue for motion pictures, the only works he created for the stage between 1932 and 1952 were collaborative efforts with established playwrights. After the belated and critically successful premiere of *Three Top Hats* in 1952, he began to direct his talents more purposefully to playwriting. He has since produced an impressive series of humoristic dramatic works that bear the unmistakable imprint of his comic style. He has also regularly served as director of his own plays, rewriting and altering the original scripts during production.

In 1943 Mihura wrote an introduction for an edition of *Three Top Hats* published some eight years before the play was first seen on the stage.[29] This autobiographical essay is essential reading for all who seek a better understanding of the creative process in the theater. It is a beautifully written tribute to the stage which reminds us that the theater is an amalgam—which consists of actors, directors, elements of chance, and personal passion as well as dialogue, poetry, inspiration, and talent—and suggests that masterpieces are not likely to be created outside the theatrical mainstream and the kind of fermentation that accompanies the bringing-to-life of a dramatic work. Commenting on the circumstances of his birth into the bosom of the theater, he noted:

I am the son of an actor, and I have always been proud of it. I believe that in life there are two classes of people: spectators and actors. Those who pay for seeing and those who collect for letting themselves be seen. The lion and those who form a chorus on the other side of the grating looking at the lion. And it has always seemed to me that the lion is the cleverest of the group.[30]

He tells us further that *Three Top Hats* came into existence rather by chance (though perhaps one should read a number of Mihura's plays before taking this statement literally), and he indicates that the inspiration for the comedy was his own short-lived participation in a theatrical troupe which was touring the Spanish provinces. And, of course, his unexpected illness provided the time for the actual composition.

The action of *Three Top Hats* is limited in space to a bedroom of a second-class provincial hotel and in time to a period of a few hours. The principal character, a young man named Dionisio (an ironic name in the light of his sexual inexperience), arrives to spend the final night of freedom before his marriage into a staid and conservative family. The sole redeeming feature of the hotel is its view of the sea (a poetic touch Mihura would again employ in his plays), but for a while it becomes the setting for a bizarre celebration by members of a touring theater company. Dionisio becomes enamored of Paula, a pretty member of Buby Barton's Ballet and Buby's girl friend. (Buby is black, as was a member of the company Mihura toured with before writing the work, and in the *autocrítica* which appeared at the time of the premiere the playwright expressed regret that he turned out to be an unlikeable character.)[31] Other persons who wander on the scene are identified with names such as "The Odious Man," "The Handsome Young Man," and "The Happy Explorer"; and there is a bearded lady known as Madame Olga.

The attractiveness of the make-believe world, enhanced by champagne, causes Dionisio to have second thoughts about marriage to a small-town girl who has twelve moles and whom he has never kissed. He confides to Paula:

DIONISIO. . . . I had a feeling that getting married was ridiculous. . . . Now I see that I wasn't wrong. I was getting married because I have spent my life stuck in a dreary little town, and I thought that to be happy I had to get married to the first girl who made my heart beat with tenderness when we looked into each other's eyes. I adored my fiancée. . . . But now I see that the happiness I was looking for doesn't have anything to do with my fiancée. . . .

I didn't know anything about anything. I only knew how to stroll and whistle next to the bandstand. . . . I was getting married because everyone always gets married when they're twenty-seven. . . . But now I'm not going to get married, Paula. . . . I can't eat fried eggs at six-thirty in the morning![32]

He asks Paula to run away with him to find adventure but she declines. After telling him the realities of her own life, she sends Dionisio off to a conventional (and dull) existence. A door has been opened only momentarily to give the young man a glimpse of the unconventional and of the special magic of illusion. But Mihura has not failed to show us that escape does not bring happiness automatically. Behind the allurement of play-acting and the excitement of imagination unleashed there may be tawdriness and sadness. In the words of Paula an undercurrent of despair can be detected, and we know that she suffers the frequent abuse of Buby.

In their introduction to the textbook edition of a later Mihura play *(Mi adorado Juan)*, Falconieri and Pasquariello have written perceptively of the playwright's theater, and they have noted his somewhat Chaplinesque version of life and its relationships.[33] Although Dionisio does not show any strong resemblance to the little clown himself, there is undeniably something of the Chaplin pathos in his fumbling and in his failure to find his love for Paula reciprocated. *Three Top Hats* is a sad absurdist farce. The special blend of the ridiculous and the pathetic, of gaiety and melancholy, and the subtle suggestions of the unresolvable contradictions in human experience make this play an extraordinary theatrical creation. José Monleón lists the play with Buero's *Story of a Stairway* and Sastre's *Condemned Squad* as a work of unusual historical importance in the Spanish theater of the last thirty years.[34] It is conceivable that *Three Top Hats* may prove to be the most enduring of the three in terms of dramatic viability.

In 1953 three new works by Mihura were seen in Madrid. *El caso de la señora estupenda* (The Case of the Stupendous Lady) was an unabashed spoof of the conventional plays of intrigue or spy dramas, with clever turns of events and the unexpected shifts of thought (often illogical) which were to become typical devices in the playwright's comedies. At times the play brings to mind John Huston's American film *Beat the Devil*, which also makes light of an overly exploited genre. However, *Stupendous Lady* does not as a whole represent the dramatist at his best, despite its undeniable entertainment value. *Una mujer cualquiera* (Any Woman Will do), which was staged a few months later, is an atypical Mihura work and probably his least interesting effort. It is a serious murder mystery with melodramatic twists and coincidences and no suggestion of mockery, humor, or satire. A *media luz los tres* (Three in Dim Light), first performed in November, 1953, was the most successful of the three. Though hardly profound and not representative of Mihura's most accomplished writing, it is nevertheless a comic *tour de force* in which one actress (Conchita Montes in the original production) plays all four female roles.

Mihura's sole offering in 1954, *El caso del señor vestido de violeta* (The Case of the Gentleman Dressed in Violet), was an outlandish theatrical escapade with comic situations and devices that strongly recall the plays of Jardiel Poncela. The principal character (Roberto) is a sensitive bullfighter who reads Schopenhauer to "get his mind off things" and who suffers from an improbable "little old lady complex." Since he actually takes on the manner and voice of his lost grandmother from time to time, he has a special room provided for his attacks. Expectedly, the secret of the room is exploited for its full suspense value. There are cases of multiple identity, such as that of "Miss Denis," whose real name is Dionisia and who speaks with a humorous Andalusian accent, and passages of genuine absurdist dialogue. Perhaps it would not be unfair to say that the play contains extravagances of action and dialogue that could best be described as Spanish camp. However, the real problem with *The Case of the Gentleman Dressed in Violet* has little to do with the quality of the comic inspiration but results rather from a marked decrease in dramatic interest in the final act. The opening act is excellent, and the second does not fail to sustain interest in the remarkable "case," but the final resolution is clumsy and conventional (after a highly unconventional buildup which leads the audience to expect more than is forthcoming). The comedy ends happily when Roberto finds his lost grandmother and regains the love of his girl friend (as well as his "real" identity).

In 1955 Mihura produced a new work that was more representative of his talents. *Sublime decisión* (Sublime Decision), set at the turn of the century, is a comedy about a young woman (Florita) who instigates her own revolution for women's rights. Her "sublime decision" is to invade a world of men with a mysterious machine called a "typewriter." While this play may not seem particularly forceful when viewed purely as a document on female liberation, Mihura's satire of the male superiority complex and the force of social convention is both trenchant and devastating. But what elevates *Sublime Decision* above the level of mere entertainment and clever satire is the note of questioning that underlies Florita's ultimate victory.

This comedy also represents Mihura's attempts to achieve a more flexible dramatic structuring in his work. The play opens with a type of prologue spoken offstage by the protagonist, and the action is repeatedly interrupted or broken off by comments and résumés. (Mihura cautions against the use of tapes for these speeches.) In the opening section, Florita hints at the nature of her "decision" but does not disclose it. Then the main curtain opens to reveal a second hanging which is painted to represent the front of a modest old dwelling. Immediately we have a typical example of Mihuran whimsy: an abandoned child is in a basket at the doorway—not a surprising occurrence in midwinter, according to Florita. Two older men who will appear later in act 2 simply walk by. In a moment Doña Rosa, Florita's mother, appears and pushes the basket aside with her cane. Florita's voice continues to comment on events of the day until the second curtain disappears to reveal the parlor of her home.

A remarkable absurdist scene follows. Three pairs of women are gossiping and relating trivia, but the audience understands only wisps of the dialogue at most and cannot create any logical meaning from it. Individuals change conversation partners, always managing to end up talking to the character most distant (preventing any suggestion of intimacy). It is a splendid piece of orchestrated nonsense. The next scene is also a fine example of comic invention. Florita's sister (Cecilia) is expecting a gentleman caller, and the family busily "sets the stage" for a "drama" that has little to do with the realities of their home life. A cat has been borrowed from the concierge and sedated so that it will sleep peacefully in the lap of Don José, the father. Aunt Matilde will provide a mood of refined gentility by playing Chopin on the piano. Instead of one caller, two arrive; and both eagerly devour the hors-d'oeuvres which the family had obtained (with some difficulty) to impress the potential suitor. In truth it is a room full of destitute people feigning the blasé indifference of the rich. To the distress of her family, Florita refuses to participate in the charade.

In act 2 the young woman arrives at the incredibly mismanaged government office where she is to be permitted to work as an "experiment." Her first day's assignment is to write six names and addresses on six envelopes—a succinct indication of her superior's opinion of a woman's abilities. But Florita has also brought a new invention with her, a "pluma sin fin" (an "endless pen" or fountain pen). In spite of the initial opposition and the unconcealed contempt of the male establishment, she quickly improves the efficiency and ambience of the office. However, the supervisor decides that his experiment has not been a success (or that it has been all too successful) and Florita must give up her job. At home the typewriter sits in the parlor, like some strange work of sculpture, in place of the piano, which has been sold. Although Florita's suitor (Pablo) could provide the conventional solution of marriage, the continual changes in the government (and resultant shifts of employees) keep him in a precarious financial situation. Eventually Florita is asked to take over a newly established post for the recruitment of women workers. She finds eager candidates in her own sister and in her friends. As she begins to write down pertinent information, the material is already resembling a dossier. Pablo looks on helplessly as Florita's liberation becomes certain.

Sublime Decision is one of Mihura's better comedies; and it is a play with a degree of social commentary even though the action is removed in time from contemporary events. The ending is not a conventionally happy one despite the dialogue that is aimed at laughter and a situation that borders on farce. Florita looks triumphantly toward the future, but the playwright succeeds in showing that triumph can require a forfeit. As the protagonist's new power begins to solidify, we sense the setting-in of an unfortunate dehumanization.

Mi adorado Juan (My Beloved Juan), which won for Mihura the National Prize for Drama in 1956, is also a play of genuine literary and theatrical interest which can best be classified as a serious comedy. In its treatment of a highly intelligent and professionally trained man who becomes a "dropout" from a mechanized and overly formalized society, it anticipates a social phenomenon that was to become much more familiar a decade after the composition of the play. But Falconieri and Pasquariello maintain that Juan is not what was formerly known as a "beatnik" or a derider of tradition. "Juan and his odd friends symbolize man's eternal desire for expanded horizons, for the widest explorations of man's possibilities."[35] Juan rejects routine, conformity, and, particularly, the belief that hard work and dedication are virtues in themselves. He comes to love the daughter (Irene) of a celebrated scientist (Doctor Palacios) and somewhat reluctantly marries her. Irene, too, is rebelling against the constraints of her own upbringing and is willing to leave behind the comforts of middle-class life to live in a flat that overlooks the harbor.

Doctor Palacios represents the ambitious, educated man who has found his place in society and who considers that his contributions are of enduring benefit to mankind. He is now attempting to perfect a drug that will eliminate the need for men to "waste" hours sleeping. This provides the focal point for an effective contrasting of two opposing views of life (the doctor's and Juan's). Mihura uses juxtaposition of attitudes again when he shows us that Juan's decision to walk out-of-step with society had been taken with a realistic understanding of the implications of his action, whereas Irene's flight from reality was colored by romantic illusions. The married existence of the couple is hardly blissful when the irritations of life in Juan's lower-class neighborhood begin to destroy Irene's illusions. But finally a general compromise brings father, daughter, and son-in-law together. Irene steals and destroys her father's formula, Juan agrees to rejoin society as a general practitioner among the poor, and Doctor Palacios abandons his projects to live with them. For all its insights, *My Beloved Juan* ultimately avoids the harsher possibilities of its theme. The compromise ending—while neither completely illogical nor incredible—is disappointing in a work of this quality and seems contrived to tie up the story nicely. The play contains much evidence of the superior dramatic talents of Miguel Mihura but it also provides an example for the critics who accuse him of compromising those talents.

   Carlota (1957) and *Melocotón en almíbar* (Peaches and Syrup, 1958) are prime demonstrations of Mihura's skill in creating detective or crime plays that are exceptionally involved as well as highly entertaining and amusing. *Carlota* presents a clever use of suspense, calculated enigma, deft manipulation of clues, and humoristic dialogue; but the play is more than a mere diversion. It is a work of considerable artistry even though it cannot be called transcendental or profound. And in its use of flashbacks and flash-forwards it represents some of Mihura's most accomplished dramatic structuring. In her introduction to the textbook edition of *Carlota,* the editor expresses all-out enthusiasm for the play: "The construction . . . is faultless. A double but parallel plane of actions contains drama, satire, realism, and delightful caricature. It is a poetic and complicated drama developed within the rigorous laws of realism."[36] But the "realism" of *Carlota* is by no means conventional. For example, Mihura knows quite well that there is a basic nonreality and even absurdity in having Spanish actors speak Spanish in a play set in England and of a style so artificial and so universally associated with the British. He deals with this absurdity ingeniously in his opening scene by reversing languages. The first lines of dialogue are in English when a Spanish visitor in London asks one of the

"English" characters directions to a certain street. The twist is that the character who is supposed to be Spanish speaks perfect English and those who are English then go on to speak perfect Spanish. The humor of this reversal of tongues would, of course, be entirely lost in translation. *Carlota* is no mere imitation of the British mystery genre—though it evidences an almost mathematical understanding of the construction of the plays of Agatha Christie, Emlyn Williams, and other cultivators of the suspense drama. What Mihura actually does is to appropriate the devices and turn them inside out. The ending of the comedy-mystery is decidedly macabre, and one major question about the late protagonist is left unanswered—in keeping with the enigmatic nature of Carlota herself.

Whereas *Carlota* is a mystery parody with an English flavor, *Peaches and Syrup* is a zany, suspenseful comedy which offers farcical crime in the Spanish manner. The work also contains its share of the absurdist and illogical humor that is characteristic of Mihura's writing. However, the most memorable feature is the character of Sister Mary of the Angels, whose dialogue reveals a special mixture of astuteness and naiveté (perhaps feigned) and who successfully manipulates a conspicuous flowerpot filled with jewels. Marquerie attributes the inspiration for *Peaches and Syrup* to Father Brown and Miss Marple of Agatha Christie's works (or at least the inspiration for Sister Mary, the nun-nurse who becomes a detective);[37] but there are also obvious antecedents in the plays of Jardiel Poncela for the band of amateur thieves with double identities who are frustrated by an enigmatic nun.

With *Maribel y la extraña familia* (Maribel and the Strange Family), which opened on September 28, 1959, Mihura achieved his greatest popular success of the 1950's. The play ran for more than a thousand performances and received the National Prize for Drama. Subsequently it was translated into several languages and enjoyed additional success as a motion picture. This well-constructed comedy about a young prostitute from the Gran Vía whose past is erased (or ignored) by a timid widower (Marcelino) from the provinces has a frankly sentimental appeal that accounts for its extraordinary success with the public.

The opening scene of *Maribel*, which introduces the strange aunt (who shows her modernity by listening to Elvis Presley records) and her paid visitors, bears a noticeable resemblance to certain scenes of López Rubio's *The Blindfold* where the aunt and uncle enliven their existence by attracting callers through flagrantly deceitful advertisements. Later, elements of the bizarre or whimsical are again introduced in the description of the drowning of Marcelino's fat wife. However, the play remains for the most part reasonably close to a more conventional plane of reality (albeit a poetic one). The most amusing scenes are those in which Maribel's three co-workers (Nini, Pili, and Rufi) appear. During his career Mihura came to favor groups of three in his plays (three pairs of gossipers in *Sublime Decision* and, later, a trio of prostitutes in *Las entretenidas* and another of local girls in *La bella Dorotea*). With the three ladies of the night and their encounter with the world of respectability the playwright has a field day, as their Gran Vía slang meshes with the polite language of another era. *Maribel and the Strange Family* comes precariously close to being maudlin at times, but it is redeemed by its crisp humor and the poetic rewriting of truth that makes the heroine eligible for a new life.

In *El chalet de Madame Renaud* (Madame Renaud's Chalet, 1961), Mihura returned to a more whimsical and outlandish vein. This rather trivial comedy about the twice-widowed and thrice-divorced Monique Renaud, lately of Zaragoza, and her plot to solve her financial plight is frequently amusing. But when the intrigue runs out, the playwright brings in a quick solution in the form of a windfall from Spain, and the play ends with madame and two of her destitute gentlemen friends living in an innocent *ménage à trois* on the Riviera. *Las entretenidas* (Ladies of the Night, 1962) is a far more important play. Although not as well received as several other Mihura works of the 1960's, it is nevertheless an excellent serious comedy with the carefully measured humor and the current of sadness which are characteristic of his best work. Fany, the protagonist of *Ladies of the Night*, is a close theatrical relative of Maribel—though certainly not a copy. She has already found love, and for four years she has maintained a relationship with José, a forty-year-old bachelor. The differences in their backgrounds become more clearly defined and create conflicts. José grows restless and as an excuse for reclaiming his independence he expresses concern about how he is viewed by society.

Fany threatens suicide if José leaves her. It is a game she has played and won before, but Mihura suggests that the danger of miscalculation and the possibility of genuine tragedy exist. José finally devises an elaborate deception involving a fictitious pregnant fiancée from Valencia in order to escape from his ménage with Fany. But the plan creates unexpected counter-measures, and ultimately José realizes his need for genuine affection and companionship. He and Fany resume their relationship on a note of hope but with no real assurances of permanence despite Fany's illusions of a lifelong love.

The playwright derives some delectable comedy from Fany's passion for oriental decor and from the views of her friends in the "profession"—Sofi, Feli, and Pili—who resemble the three companions of Maribel. Mihura's ladies of the night are wise or naive, sentimental or caustic, but never vicious. Their language is based on the slang of the prostitute but molded by the playwright toward humoristic theatrical ends. Fany is an attractive character and more complex than Maribel. The probable reason for her story's failure to attract the same public interest as her predecessor's is that her struggle not to lose the companionship of a man she loves does not end in the kind of automatic respectability that enabled a conservative audience to accept Maribel and to overlook the implications of her immorality.

Several leading Spanish critics are in agreement that *La bella Dorotea (The Fair Dorothea, 1963)* is Mihura's finest achievement since *Three Top Hats*. Without question this appealing play ranks among the playwright's most original and most consummate works. In a number of Mihura's comedies the farcical situations are admittedly contrived and, along with the irresistible but extravagant dialogue, seem to be an end in themselves rather than an essential part of a dramatic whole. All the parts fit in *The Fair Dorothea*, and humor and pathos are blended for telling theatrical effect.

The action of the play takes place in the imaginary seaside town of Zolitzola in northern Spain, in "any year before the First World War." But the locale is really the universal small town with its limited possibilities for self-realization. Three young women of the town (Benita, Inés, and Remedios), who serve as a "chorus" to introduce the action of the play, are seated in the parlor of Don Manuel on the wedding day of his only daughter

(Dorothea). Dressed in black and carrying umbrellas, they have appeared at the improbable hour of six-fifteen in the morning, while a fierce thunderstorm is in progress. Their absurdist dialogue about the eternal rain in a town which the inhabitants view as a potential tourist attraction is not only funny but also underscores the oppressive monotony of their existence.

Then, one by one, the inhabitants of the house—Don Manuel (half-dressed), Doña Rita, the aunt (in a robe), and the servant girl Rosa—enter the parlor to search for something in a dresser drawer. They greet the three young women casually, as if they were regular fixtures and their appearance before daybreak routine. When Dorothea appears, she pretends to have slept soundly for ten hours. In the ensuing dialogue we learn that she has had difficulties in finding a suitor who would be interested in her for reasons other than her father's money. But Fermín, her husband-to-be, seems to be different.

The women in black depart, and Dorothea puts on her wedding dress—in vain, as it turns out. A note from Fermín informs the bride that everyone is saying that he is marrying her for her money and that to avoid public opprobrium he is calling off the marriage. To the distress of her family, Dorothea announces that she will go into town in her wedding attire and seek a substitute:

DOROTHEA. This very minute I'm going to look for another fiancé on the Calle Real. And I assure you that I'll return with one. If it's not this morning, it will be this evening. If it's not today, it will be tomorrow. But I'll come back with one and go to the church. Tell the priest not to go away. Have them all wait for me, for I'll be back.

DOÑA RITA. But you're going to make a fool of yourself, Dorothea.

DOROTHEA. Haven't I done that already? Aren't they all going to laugh at me? Didn't the boy who brought the letter laugh? Well, I'll laugh at them too, as I walk down the streets in my white dress looking for another man. They'll see that I'm not afraid. . . .

DOÑA RITA. You have to conform. . . . You can't be so rebellious.

DOROTHEA. I am who I am, and there's nothing more to be said.[38]

In his review of *The Fair Dorothea* for *Pueblo*, Marquerie suggested that the play should be called Doña Quijota. "Just as the Knight of the Sad Countenance sallied forth through the fields of La Mancha . . . disguised as a knight errant . . . the protagonist of this delightful theatrical work strolls through the streets of her native town dressed in a hardly customary manner . . . and is taken for a lunatic and for a rebel."[39] And later we find that Rosa, loyal and realistic, represents Dorothea's Sancho Panza in the manner in which she complements the single-minded young woman.

The second scene of the play takes place at dusk in a park, with the sea as a background and the sounds of music and a street carnival floating in from the distance. Dorothea's search has now lasted for six months and she is still wearing her wedding dress. She comes across a newcomer named Juan Bermúdez who elicits an explanation for her bizarre attire. Although her father has died and she is now looked upon as a lunatic, she has continued to face the ridicule of the townspeople. Bermúdez is from the outside world, presently operating a merry-go-round at the carnival. Unknown to Dorothea, her matter-of-fact relation of how she is now caught in her own "madness" is overheard by José Rivadavia, a sometime operetta star for whom Bermúdez acts as manager. Rosa turns up too, and when her mistress continues her stroll, she remains with Juan (whom she had actually met three days earlier). Juan has heard the story of the rich madwoman, and he has concocted a plan to have José Rivadavia marry her to acquire money to start a new theater company. Rosa is merely useful for his scheme.

In the second act the scene is shifted to the inn that Dorothea has inherited from her father. Inés, Remedios, and Benita are again on hand with their umbrellas and their preoccupation with the weather. They inform Doña Rita that they have been delegated by the women of the town to deliver to Dorothea an ultimatum: desist or suffer the consequences. José Rivadavia enters dressed in tails and top hat—both somewhat the worse for wear. He inquires about the trains that come through Zolitzola because he likes to wave at the passengers to make them happy even if he isn't himself. He rushes out to watch a train that is coming into the station, and Dorothea recognizes a kindred spirit. In outlandish theatrical style he declares that he is dressed in tails because his bride-to-be abandoned him at church. He asks Dorothea her name and tells her that she reminds him of a poem about a sad girl named Theodora. He then recites the lengthy poem to prove his point. When he goes on to propose, Dorothea surprises him by announcing that she knows he is playing a game because she has seen him in town in other attire. José admits this, but Dorothea asks him to stay. They kiss, and José helps her take off her wedding dress (the symbol of her "madness").

In the final scene the inn has become more colorful. Six weeks have passed and Rosa and Juan Bermúdez are now married. The three "friends" arrive to find out what kind of relationship exists between Dorothea and José. When Remedios pointedly asks what José does besides put up decorations, Dorothea's answer is quick. "He sleeps with me, he loves me, we sit in silence or we laugh together, and we don't worry about people."[40] The "friends" hint that this happiness won't last. When they leave, Dorothea confesses her fear that José really will be leaving that day—or if not that day, it will be the next. She has found a train ticket to Madrid in his pocket but did not manage to read the date. José does not abandon her, and he provides an elaborate explanation of why the ticket had been in his possession. It had been bought for the husband of an ex-soprano called Charito Porcholes. He has a plan to build a new inn on a plot of ground overlooking the sea where La Porcholes, and perhaps he himself, can again hear the applause of the public. How much of José's story is true and how much is invention is uncertain. But since he has found hope through Dorothea, he returns faith and illusion to her. Significantly, the new inn is to be called "The Fair Dorothea." Like *Ladies of the Night*, the play ends with the reaffirmation of a relationship without guarantees.

Mihura's greatest popular success of the 1960's came in 1964 with *Ninette y un señor de Murcia* (Ninette and a Gentleman from Murcia) a fresh and original comedy about a young Murcian bachelor (Andrés), who suddenly finds himself heir to a comfortable income and decides to spend two weeks in Paris for the purpose of having an adventure with a French girl. Looking for a *pensión* where Spanish is spoken, he quickly finds himself in the bosom of a Spanish Communist family in exile who decorate their walls with photographs of Lenin and Pablo Iglesias. Andrés experiences more than mere sexual adventure *a la française*. He is seduced by Ninette, the vivacious daughter of the expatriot Pierre (who works for Citroën), and reluctantly renounces his bachelor state when Ninette announces she is pregnant. Although her father's political views may be far to the left, he has retained the most traditional Spanish ideas on honor and marriage.

For the first time in his career as a playwright Mihura injects a measure of political satire into his dialogue, as well as humor based on specific sexual matters. Admittedly, his Communists are capitalists at heart, but audiences doubtless welcomed the opportunity to have even a humorous view of the Spaniard who lives in exile (quite successfully) because of his political convictions. *Ninette* also offers more character development and psychological insight than most of Mihura's plays; and there is a liberal use of lines spoken directly to the audience. The comedy opens with a prologue in which Andrés explains to the public about the death of his aunt and the other circumstances surrounding his arrival in Paris. In the course of the action, he also breaks out of scenes to give his interpretation of a situation or to rush the action ahead with a summary of events.

Mihura was awarded the Calderón de la Barca Prize for *Ninette,* and two years later he returned to his highly successful story to provide a continuation entitled *"Ninette," Modas de París* ("Ninette," Paris Fashions). Sequels to successful dramatic works are fairly common in the Spanish theater, but more often than not they turn out to be sadly inferior efforts that lack the esprit, the timeliness, or the fundamental artistic virtues that accounted for the appeal of the original plays. But Mihura was more fortunate in repeating success than some of his contemporaries. Though somewhat less cohesive than its predecessor, the second "Ninette" play is an excellent comic entertainment in its own right, with a sharp satirical view of the hypocrisies and contradictions of life in a provincial Spanish city. On returning to Murcia with Andrés, Ninette has suffered a miscarriage, eliminating the original reason for the marriage. After a taste of married life, Andrés develops a new romantic interest and Ninette must use her wits to regain his devotion. The title of the play refers to a boutique specializing in Paris fashions that Ninette decides to open in Murcia. Her father and mother have also returned to the native soil, and much of the humor is based on their readjustment to the "new" Spain. Eventually Andrés joins forces with his father-in-law to open a Citroën agency in Murcia, and Ninette has the child she yearns for. The playwright also retains in the second *Ninette* the device of speeches directed to the audience to supply résumés and personal views of the two principal characters.

Other Mihura plays of the 1960's are *Milagro en casa de los*

López (Miracle at the López House, Barcelona, 1964; Madrid, 1965), *La tetera* (The Teapot, 1965), *La decente* (A Real Lady, 1967), and *Sólo el amor y la luna traen fortuna* (Only Love and the Moon Bring Good Luck, 1968). All of these works follow familiar lines of development and contain types of humor and suspense characteristic of the playwright's earlier writing. All four fall generally into the category of the suspense or mystery genre. None adds any new dimension to Mihura's art. A drama critic for *ABC* summed up the virtues of *Only Love and the Moon Bring Good Luck* in a statement that might well serve for other lesser comedies by Mihura: "A minor comedy, a piece of evasion aimed at laughter, without other ambitions. It is an exercise by an author who, because of the richness of his verbal keyboard, can compose a sonatina with the lightest, the shortest, the most insignificant melody."[41]

Rarely has a writer repeated himself so successfully as Miguel Mihura without evoking monotony or an excessive sense of *déjà vu*. He has not been an innovator in terms of dramatic form, for, with the exception of occasional use of commentaries and prologues delivered by a single character to the audience and of flashbacks and flash-forwards in *Carlota*, there are no departures from what could be termed the most conventional dramatic structure. It is in the skillful linking of humor, absurdism, pathos, and suspense that his artistic talent is most evident. Frequently his humor is illogical[42] and highly unconventional, derived from a remarkable sensitivity to word use, sound, interpretations, and verbal suggestions. The juxtaposition of opposites is a common recourse both in his plotting and in his comic dialogue. Like Ionesco, Mihura is keenly aware of the small (and often pathetic) rituals that serve as human communication and points up their absurdities. And like López Rubio he is quick to turn a dramatic cliché to a new and unexpected theatrical purpose. His special type of humor (also displayed in the magazine *La Codorniz*) can be linked to that of the late Enrique Jardiel Poncela, but some of the similarity is based on common associations with the long Spanish tradition of humor and a shared view of the absurd, rather than imitation. Mihura is to a degree an absurdist, but strictly speaking he does not write theater of the absurd. The vignettes of the absurd in his plays are generally tied to passages of a more conventional nature, in which sentimentality often comes to the fore. In many instances the plots of the playwright's comedies are so involved that they defy any kind of meaningful résumé. Only first-hand contact with such works can truly show that such intricacies have a satisfying dramatic purpose. In his most memorable plays—from *Three Top Hats* to *The Fair Dorothea*—Mihura deals with the tantalizing attractions that life sometimes offers to awaken our ideals and inspire our illusions and the impossibility of achieving a full realization of such illusions. One might accuse Mihura of creating a capricious world that denies the realities of contemporary society, but that would indicate a failure to grasp the essence of his theater. For it is in that very capriciousness that the predicaments of man are frequently illuminated in his plays.

III *Joaquin Calvo-Sotelo*

Joaquin Calvo-Sotelo was born on March 5, 1905, in La Coruña, a city on the coast of Spain's northwest corner. During his childhood he lived in other parts of the country and, like López Rubio, he completed the final years of his education in Madrid. Looking forward to a career in government (his father had been a civil servant and his brother José was to become the leader of the conservative forces in the *Cortes* during the Spanish Republic, subsequently to be assassinated in 1936 on the eve of the outbreak of the civil war), he obtained a degree in law in 1926. Calvo-Sotelo's interest in writing predated his recognition as a playwright, and he had already attracted some attention as a journalist for *A B C* before his first dramatic work was performed in 1930. During the period of the republic and the war years he wrote intermittently for the stage. In 1937 he went to Chile as a political exile and also traveled extensively in Asia and North America for several years. In the mid-1940's he began to create theater more actively and by 1949 his career as a playwright was in full flower. That year his sentimental comedy *La visita que no tocó el timbre* (The Caller Who Didn't Ring) was warmly received by the public and was awarded the Jacinto Benavente Prize for the best play of the season. (Both Buero-Vallejo's *Story of a Stairway* and López Rubio's *Celos del aire* had been appropriately honored by other theatrical awards during the same season.) Over the next two years, five plays by Calvo-Sotelo were staged either in Madrid or Barcelona. His career reached its peak in 1954 with the thesis drama of conscience *La muralla* (The Wall), which attracted unusual public and critical acclaim; and in 1955 he was elected to membership in the Royal Spanish Academy. Calvo-Sotelo continued to be remarkably productive into the 1960's. By cannily varying his thematic material, alternating comedies with serious plays and occasional off-beat dramas, while gauging the public mood of the moment, he also maintained his popularity with an influential segment of Spanish theater audiences.

The Caller Who Didn't Ring is an amusing and, at times, affecting comedy—not unlike the type of humorous theater that Neil Simon began to cultivate so successfully in the United States some years later. The plot is minimal: two middle-aged brothers (Santiago and Juan), whose protective mother has died and left them without a real family, find an abandoned infant at their door one morning. The only identification is a recording on which the mother has given the baby's name (Santiaguito) and a brief statement of her hopes for his future. The brothers first attempt to rid themselves of the unwanted "caller who didn't ring" by placing the bundle in front of a neighbor's door; but the child is quickly and humorously returned to them. Because of their bachelor existence, they know nothing of caring for a baby. When he begins to cry, it does not occur to them that he is simply hungry. In desperation they call a doctor who sends over his pretty young nurse (Emma). When Emma arrives, the brothers (and the audience) mistake her for the child's mother. Later the real mother calls and her melodramatic story is repeated by Juan as she relates it by phone. At the mother's request, the baby is returned the way he arrived. He is simply left outside the door so that the mother can return unseen and pick him up. In a matter of hours Santiago and Juan have become attached to little Santiaguito, but the possible pathos of the situation is quickly avoided by two telephone calls: one announcing that the pretty nurse is coming back and that she will bring her twin sister; and the second from the mother assuring them that all is well and that some time in the future she will bring the child for a proper visit.

Although *The Caller Who Didn't Ring* is clearly escapist fare, the skillful play of dialogue between the two brothers who are physically almost identical but psychologically somewhat different raises the work above the level of the routine in certain passages. And the humor derived from their comments on everyday Spanish life, the unfortunate state of journalism in Spain circa 1950, and the contrasts between American and peninsular mores (a much-mined source of humor in contemporary Spanish comedy) is quite piquant. The use of a recorded message from the mother rather than the traditional note that always accompanies abandoned infants is an excellent touch that is exploited by the author for maximum theatrical effect. However, the final act of the play is weak, marred by the cliché-filled tale of illegitimacy related by the unseen mother and repeated verbatim by Juan for the benefit of Santiago and the audience, and by the too facile mention of the nurse's twin sister which leaves the implication that Santiago and Juan will find belated domestic bliss with the two young women. In short, a potentially moving commentary on age and loneliness is avoided in favor of an implied happy ending.

When *Criminal de guerra* (War Criminal) had its Barcelona premiere in 1951, following the successful Madrid production, one critic expressed the opinion that the play was "an imperishable work that will figure in the anthologies of theater through the years."[43] Some twenty years later such a prediction seems naive, for the treatment of a theme that was undeniably timely and meaningful is neither original nor penetrating enough to give *War Criminal* enduring significance. This moralistic thesis drama represents one pole of Calvo-Sotelo's dramatic interests but it is far from the best of his plays of this genre. While it is a sincerely felt expression of the playwright's antiwar sentiments, it attempts to deal with the complex problem of German war guilt without paying more than token recognition to the documented horrors of Nazism.

The action takes place in Germany at the end of World War II and is concerned with an American officer (William Kennerlein) of German descent who finds himself in charge of the prosecution of a German general (Hoffmann) who is accused of ordering the execution of twenty prisoners of war. Hoffmann's wife is actually a blood relative of Kennerlein, and her daughter (Elizabeth) had visited the American branch of the family before the war. After the general has been condemned to death, it is discovered that the order for the killing of the prisoners had been signed by the police and not by the military. However, before a reprieve can be obtained, Hoffman commits suicide. Ironically, it was the American Kennerlein who supplied him with the poison so that he could avoid the humiliation of being hanged. Elizabeth has felt love for Kennerlein since she first knew him in the United States, and at the end of the play she is still able to admit her love even though the American provided the means for her father's death. Kennerlein becomes spokesman for the dramatist when he declares:

KENNERLEIN. . . . We have all comitted crimes. Those of you who declared war because of your ambitions and those of us who demand . . . unconditional surrender. Those who bombed Coventry and those who destroyed Hiroshima. Those who murdered . . . Jews by the thousands and those who set fire to the ancient cathedrals.[44]

Both sides are shown to be "war criminals"—an idea that is not rejected today in the United States—and the German military "aristocracy" is depicted as capable of traditional honor in spite of their support of the Nazi regime.

In essence *War Criminal* is an old-fashioned, three-act melodrama, at times bombastic in tone; all the action is confined to the traditional stage living room, with a stairway designed for effective entrances. The exposition is labored and painfully obvious (a flaw that is apparent in other works of the author), and the German contingent of characters is assigned an array of postures to reinforce the argumentative and frequently artificial dialogue. In its totality the play seems divorced from the stark realities of its time.

In 1952, Calvo-Sotelo's *Maria Antonieta* (Marie Antoinette) represented a departure—both technically and thematically—from the dramas of moralistic tone and the humorous works that constitute the greater part of his writing in the 1950's. While hardly a masterpiece, and notably flawed, *Marie Antoinette* remains an intriguing little drama and is perhaps a clearer indication of its author's inventiveness than some of his more acclaimed efforts of those years. The play is divided into seven fairly brief scenes which take place in Paris and Versailles in the present, though the past is fundamental to the development of the plot. The conventional, realistic setting used almost exclusively in Spanish theaters at the time is abandoned in favor of a bare stage on which a minimum of properties is employed to suggest the various locations and situations—such as a public square, a modern apartment, and the Trianon Palace. Each scene is given a title in the printed script in the manner of many plays of the past century.

In the opening scene, Pierre de Armigny, a wealthy Frenchman, and his friend Jaime Serrat, a young Spanish attaché, are standing late at night in the Place de la Concorde. Unable to find a taxi, they begin to talk about the events of the French Revolution that took place where they are waiting, particularly the execution of Marie Antoinette. The two men are amazed to see a young woman, dressed in the attire in which the ill-fated queen appears in the painter David's drawing of her, walk from the shadows. When she speaks she creates the impression that she believes she is actually Marie Antoinette resurrected and uses the formal language of the eighteenth-century court. (In Spanish the "vos" form for "you" is employed.) Jaime goes along with the "game," addressing her as if she were royalty and offers her lodging in his apartment. Significantly, she asks about the fate of the Swedish Count Hans-Axel von Fersen (supposedly the lover of the queen and the planner of the aborted escape of the royal family from Versailles during the revolution). She also notes a resemblance between Jaime and Fersen. In the third scene, Paul Brecourt, a minor public official and the husband of the young woman, appears after reading a notice which Jaime has placed in several Paris newspapers. ("Mental patient, identity unknown. Believes herself to be Marie Antoinette. . . .") He explains in detail that his wife is really Susana Wiedermann, a Viennese refugee from the Nazis, and that her mania was unknown to him until after their marriage.

Jaime obtains the husband's permission to keep Susana with him to see if he can bring about the cure that doctors and drugs have not effected. At her own request, Susana is taken to Versailles, where she shows a striking familiarity with the surroundings. The most startling incident occurs when she tells of a secret drawer in a desk which is found to exist and to contain an actual letter from Fersen. Serrat's plan for curing Susana involves a reenactment in the Trianon Palace of a scene from the past in which he will portray Fersen and the housekeeper will play the part of a royal lady-in-waiting to the queen. It has been arranged for the Chief of the Guards at the palace to interrupt the "play" and to accuse all involved of illegal impersonation. The plan fails, for Susana continues to insist that she is Marie Antoinette. Seeing her anguish, Jaime returns to his role of Hans to spare her further suffering. He then conceives an elaborate scheme to convince the young woman that the present French government is demanding her second execution. Under the pretext of making a film called *It happened in Versailles*, a guillotine is set up in the Place de la Concorde. As Pierre expresses it, perhaps a "filmoshock" can achieve the effect of an "electroshock." All of the equipment for filming is set up and the action begins. Jaime begs Marie Antoinette to save herself by repeating the line: "I am Susana Wiedermann." But, dramatically, she insists on her historical identity and collapses. When she sinks to the ground, the coif falls from her head revealing that her hair is now completely gray (as Marie Antoinette's was reported to be). Susana-Marie has actually willed her own death and dies as the queen and not as Susana Wiedermann.

Marie Antoinette reveals some structural similarities to Anouilh's *Pauvre Bitos* (which was written some four years later) and Achard's *Le Corsaire* in its Pirandellian device of recreating the past and in the resulting transformation of the play-within-a-play into a new level of reality. Jaime's efforts to bring Susana-Marie back to conventional reality must, of course, be accepted as legitimate theatrical means to an end rather than the application of any serious understanding of mental derangement. For some, *Marie Antoinette* may seem little more than a suspense melodrama with a hint of the supernatural (for the discovery of the letter in the hidden drawer has no logical explanation). As for the faults of the play, Torrente Ballester has stated what he considers them to be in one of his most overwhelmingly negative evaluations of a dramatic work.[45] He finds the play lacking in eloquence that might give a degree of grandeur to the protagonist; he considers it reminiscent of Pirandello's *Enrico IV* and shamefully derivative; and he views the appearance of Susana-Marie herself as being on the ridiculous side. Quite justifiably he notes that the principal male character (Jaime) is hopelessly *cursi* ("tasteless"). Marquerie, in his summary of contemporary theater,

Veinte años de teatro en España, omits all mention of the work in his chapter on Calvo-Sotelo. Yet in retrospect it is possible to view Marie Antoinette as an interesting experiment in which the author was attempting—albeit with less than total success—to break away from the restraints of both conventional time and more traditional staging concepts at a moment when Spanish scenic design was in a state of artistic retardation.

Marie Antoinette was followed in 1953 by *La mariposa y el ingeniero* (The Butterfly and the Engineer), an ironic comedy on the familiar theme of *"El curioso impertinente"* from *Don Quixote; El jefe* (The Leader), a somber and violent drama; and *Milagro en la Plaza del Progreso* (Miracle in the Plaza del Progreso), a very successful comedy in the *sainete* tradition of popular Spanish humor. Of the three, *The Leader* attracted the most critical attention. Valbuena Prat has ranked the work close to *The Wall* among Calvo-Sotelo's plays performed prior to 1955.[46] The structure of *The Leader* is similar to that of *Marie Antoinette*, with brief, crisp scenes which generally end with a note of suspense or a violent action, though without the varied changes of locale of the earlier play and the nonliteral setting. In both instances certain similarities to a screenplay are obvious; and the suspense and intrigue pictures produced in the 1940's (especially by Warner Brothers) do come to mind when we consider *The Leader*. Not only does the principal character himself seem tailored to the talents of the late Humphrey Bogart, but the somewhat bizarre types that surround him also vaguely recall the roles played by Peter Lorre and other highly individualistic character actors. Both Torrente Ballester[47] and Francisco Ruiz Ramón[48] have noted the cinematic features of the work—the former citing the American motion picture *Key Largo* (adapted, to be sure, from a play by Maxwell Anderson) as being close in thought and mood. Torrente has also noted in his critique of the play the possible influence of Ortega y Gasset's essay "El origen deportivo del Estado," dealing with the growth of power and law, on the playwright's basic thesis: that the creation of a power center is inevitable when the common interest demands it.

In *The Leader*, Calvo-Sotelo has aspired to a more significant intellectual statement than a mere adventure drama normally contains. He is showing the need for direction and order even among the lawless if they are to survive in a hostile environment; and, ironically, it is his protagonist Anatol, an anarchist convicted of political assassination in his youth, who must assume the role of "leader." The plot deals with the efforts of a group of escaped criminals who have taken refuge on a small island to maintain control of the island's inhabitants and ultimately to escape from their new "prison." Years before, in his youthful belief in anarchism, Anatol had shot a major political figure. Now, as a fugitive from justice and accompanied by an assortment of criminals of every ilk, he realizes that he must lead. He develops a deep attachment to one of the women on the island, a young widow (Esther) who discovers the fine intellect and innate nobility of the "criminal's" character. Anatol is forced to shoot one of the islanders, a man close to Esther, who is attempting to escape to inform the authorities of the whereabouts of the fugitives. Esther herself is murdered by one of the most violent of the escapees, and at the end of the play Anatol is assassinated. His murderer then becomes the new leader.

The production of *The Wall* in 1954 resulted in exceptional acclaim for Calvo-Sotelo. The work received high critical praise at that time and enjoyed one of the longest runs of any play in the history of the Spanish theater; it was quickly translated into several languages and made into a motion picture. Even after almost two decades more of theatrical creativity by the playwright, no other play of his has achieved comparable success or surpassed *The Wall* in sheer dramatic impact. One of the reasons for the extraordinary success of the play was the fact that it considered with some frankness the tragic period of the Spanish civil war—specifically, the unjust action of a young Nationalist soldier against a leftist *rojo* ("Red") on the side of the republic. Also, the characters were present-day Spaniards rather than Europeans of some imaginary country (as in *The Leader* and, later, in *The Godless City*) or Germans and Americans speaking Spanish as in *War Criminal*. Consequently, their expression is never less than credible; and at the climax of the play the dialogue reaches a level of eloquence and telling dramatic veracity. Certain defects noted in Calvo-Sotelo's dramaturgy, such as his inability to handle exposition unobtrusively and a tendency toward melodramatic outbursts, are less conspicuous in *The Wall*, though by no means totally remedied.

The plot of this drama of conscience shows some resemblance to that of Echegaray's nineteeth-century play *O locura o santidad* (Madman or Saint). Jorge Hontanar, a successful and wealthy member of Spain's upper middle-class, suffers a heart attack; he survives but he has been shocked into an awareness of his own mortality and makes an unshakable resolution to redress a wrong of his youth. During the civil war, his godfather had been assassinated in Badajoz and had left his estate, El Tomillar, to an illegitimate son (Gervasio Quiroga). Jorge had arrived in the city with the occupying nationalist forces. In exchange for his freedom, a local republican notary changed the will so that the estate went to Jorge. Hontanar's rationalization of the action was that the property simply represented spoils of war (since Quiroga was an active *rojo*). At first Jorge's wife (Cecilia) agrees to go along with his desire to return the estate to Quiroga, but after her wisecracking, poker-playing mother confronts her with an explanation of what this will mean to their way of life, she weakens. Jorge is determinedly opposed by his daughter, the father of the daughter's fiancé, and—quite craftily—by the mother-in-law. A "wall" of opposition is raised by all who have something to lose if Hontanar obeys the dictates of his conscience. Finally, the mother-in-law makes certain that Quiroga will not be allowed to see Jorge. Helpless to overcome the wall, Jorge suffers a second attack and dies directing his final words to God rather than to his family.

The Wall is a very conventional work as far as its form is concerned, with traditional exposition and obligatory confrontation scenes (husband-wife, wife-mother, daughter-father, etc.), which are undeniably effective dramatically in spite of their obviousness. In a lengthy introductory essay which accompanies the published text of the work,[49] Calvo-Sotelo provides information on the prolonged genesis of this play as well as insight into his methods of composition. Various endings had been written including one with an epilogue in which Hontanar's wife has a change of heart and makes restitution to Quiroga after her husband's death. Almost on the eve of the opening, the definitive ending was written and rehearsed (over the objections of the producer). It is, of course, the dramatic quality of the final episode that ensures *The Wall* a high place among the author's works.

In spite of the original praise lavished on *The Wall*, subsequent critical commentary has been far from unanimously favorable. Although the play puts into focus the contradictions within a society between an official moral position and actual social practice, it does not offer any alternative to the status quo; and, as José Monleón has pointed out, such a work succeeds in gaining public approbation by permitting the audience "to resolve its moral problems without the necessity of producing any modification of social reality."[50] In a detailed analysis of *The Wall* and the causes of its popularity,[51] Jerónimo Mallo concedes that the drama is well written but does not see it as an enduring work. Rather it is a play that was timely and responsive to the attitudes and conditions of a particular moment in Spanish theatrical history. But it does not treat essential values of human existence nor does it lay bare the deepest roots of a national problem.

Following the success of *The Wall*, the playwright continued to produce varied dramatic fare for Spanish stages. *Historia de una resentido* (Story of a Resentful Man), a heavy drama about a would-be playwright who commits an act of violence during the civil war and is executed, had its premiere in Barcelona in 1955. A more important serious work, *La ciudad sin Dios* (The Godless City) was produced in January, 1957. This is an ambitious play of Pirandellian design in which an actor from a touring company is asked to portray a Christian prophet for the government of a fictitious country where applied political doctrine has eradicated religion completely over a period of fifty years. As a test, to see if the citizens are still susceptible to religious persuasion, the actor (Nicolai Nordson) goes to the atheistic city of Welskoye and begins to preach the immortality of the soul. After his third "appearance" he is arrested and put in prison for a month. Nicolai becomes enamored of his role and seems to be believing his own lines. People come to the abandoned monastery where he takes up residence; miracles are attributed to him—although he rejects any pretentions of having supernatural powers. The government leader, called the "Commissaire," decides to stage a series of miracles for the purpose of revealing them to be frauds later. Throughout the play the Commissaire functions as both playwright and director, but his "drama" becomes greater than his own concept of it. Naturally, illusion eventually becomes reality.

The first two miracles are performed according to plan, but the third—the resurrecting of a corpse—poses a problem. The man selected to play the deceased actually dies before the miracle can take place. Nicolai interprets this as a genuine act of God (a miracle in reverse) and he is converted by the experience. Now that the actor really believes himself to be a prophet with a divine mission, the Commissaire finds him useless for the purpose of exposing religion as false. He must be put away in an asylum as a madman. To free Nicolai from such a fate, his fellow-actor David kills him. As he is dying, Nicolai repeats a line of the death scene from the last play he had been performing before being tempted by the Commissaire. In a brief epilogue, a crippled girl prays at the spot where the actor died, and suddenly she rises up without the aid of her crutch (a *true* miracle).

The theme of *The Godless City* recalls particularly Luca de Tena's *¿Quién soy yo?*, in which a political leader is impersonated, and *El gesticulador*, by the Mexican playwright Rodolfo Usigli, in which a teacher takes the place of a slain revolutionary—both works equally Pirandellian in inspiration. The principal difference in Calvo-Sotelo's work is his utilization of the familiar theatrical device to develop his idea of man's fundamental yearning and need for the religious supernatural. But despite the playwright's serious intentions and the undeniable effectiveness of the opening scenes of the work, the theme eventually exceeds his grasp. Frequent speeches on acting and the nature of theater, which are designed to be intellectually provocative, become tedious in their excess and obviousness. Melodrama intrudes as Nicolai moves toward his destruction; and because of the unnecessary epilogue tacked on to the end of the play, *The Godless City* ends up seeming more like a sermon than a dramatic experience. In this work, as in several other of the author's serious dramas, the fictitious names of persons and places, which usually sound vaguely middle-European, add an annoying note of artificiality.

Four months after the premiere of *The Godless City, Una muchacha de Valladolid (A Girl From Valladolid)* opened in Madrid and ran for some four hundred performances—a substantial run by any standards. This light piece about the matrimonial problems of a young woman whose husband is in the diplomatic corps is made-to-order theater which lacks the inventiveness or the satirical bite of some of the comedies of

López Rubio and Mihura. It is padded with trivialities and is inoffensive to the point of tedium. Sainz de Robles, who included *A Girl From Valladolid* in his annual anthology of Spanish plays, noted that in a non-Spanish climate the comedy would have taken on a "vodevil" tone; but "the traditional pen of Calvo-Sotelo repudiates the old and provocative French naughtiness in favor of a scenic romp . . . flavored with . . . Spanish morality."[52] In 1960 the playwright wrote *Cartas credenciales* (Credentials of a diplomat), a truly uninspired sequel to *A Girl From Valladolid;* and two years later still another routine comedy on life in the Spanish diplomatic corps, *Operación embajada* (Operation Embassy), was produced. *Micaela,* a farcical but more substantial work based on a short novel by Juan Antonio de Zunzunegui, was also staged in 1962.

As Calvo-Sotelo continued to write prolifically in the 1960's, he did not abandon his policy of alternating light plays with more ambitious serious dramas; but, eclectic by inclination, he showed himself receptive to more modern and more flexible dramatic forms. Two of his most important accomplishments belong to this period: the historical drama *El proceso del arzobispo Carranza* (The Trial of Archbishop Carranza, 1964) and the darkly satirical *El inocente* (The Innocent Soul, 1968). Conceivably, the playwright's decision to undertake his first play based on the life of a historical personage was influenced by Buero-Vallejo's notable turn to historical theater during the years immediately preceding the composition of *Archbishop Carranza.*[53] However, it should not be concluded that Calvo-Sotelo intended to evoke comparisons with Buero's impressive dramas or to imitate the style and purpose of the younger writer. *Archbishop Carranza* lacks the visionary theme that is basic to all of Buero's plays dealing with individuals or events from the past; it also differs from Luca de Tena's two recreations of the life and times of Alfonso XII, which are romanticized and sentimental versions of history, without any challenging intellectual qualities. Calvo-Sotelo's method can be called "documentary" in that he attempts to recreate only the events and situations pertinent to the accusation of heresy against his protagonist and the subsequent struggle for absolution. There is no romantic love whatsoever in the work nor attempts to sentimentalize the relationships of the archbishop with his devoted sister and other associates. Rather the drama moves purposefully, in its five scenes covering events of some seventeen years, toward a moving ending, without digressions or slackening of dramatic momentum.

Details on the life of Fray Bartolomé de Carranza, the central character of the work, are not widely known outside of Spain. Archbishop of Toledo, primate of Spain, and spiritual advisor to Mary Tudor, he was one of Europe's leading Catholic theologians of the sixteenth century and a strong voice at the Council of Trent. In 1559 he was accused by the Spanish Inquisition of heretical writing and opinions. The instigator of the investigation was the Archbishop of Seville, a rival of Carranza's in the church hierarchy, and the accusations were based on statements taken out of context. For seventeen years Carranza endured imprisonment and interrogation in Spain and in Rome as his case moved with appalling slowness toward a final decision from the Vatican. When it appeared that the prelate might be absolved by Pius V, the Pope died and his successor, Gregory XIII, finally made a pronouncement that is described in the play as being "halfway between absolution and conviction." The Archbishop is considered "seriously suspect of heresy but not a heretic," and he is suspended from the administration of his diocese for another five years—effectively removing him from any meaningful activity for the remainder of his life. In the very moving final scene of Calvo-Sotelo's drama, death comes before the aged man can return to Spain. And even his loyal sister expresses doubts about his strict adherence to the faith. As the tick-tock of a clock reminds the audience of the slow but inexorable passing of time, the dying theologian accepts the papal decision and renounces each of the statements which had been considered to be "leaning toward Protestanism." A priest stands beside him and pronounces the Latin words of absolution.

Given Calvo-Sotelo's strong self-identification as a Catholic writer for a Catholic nation, it is understandable that he would be attracted to the case of Archbishop Carranza. The playwright obviously sympathizes with the spiritual struggle of the strong-willed churchman, but he convincingly keeps him within the faith at the end of the play. Although there is no clear indication that the author has intended to evoke mental associations between the events of *The Trial of Archbishop Carranza* and any contemporary situations, he has indeed created a work that effectively condemns the misuse of power and ideological interpretation in any age.

Only seven days after the opening of his light and ephemeral comedy *Una noche de lluvia* (A Rainy Night) in October, 1968, a surprising and memorable play by Calvo-Sotelo had its premiere. *El inocente* (The Innocent Soul), with its blunt language, its unconventional theme, and its imaginative construction, represented a type of theater unexpected from this dramatist. Despite a forced and illogical ending, *The Innocent Soul* contains some of Calvo-Sotelo's finest dramatic writing; it is also one of the most disturbing Spanish plays of the 1960's—both in what it attempts to say and in what it fails to acknowledge.

The playwright employs a modern version of the classical chorus—dressed in miniskirts and stationed apart from the actors—to introduce the theme and characters and to comment on the action in verse (which contrasts with the sometimes harsh prose of the dialogue). The "innocent soul" of the title is Dominico Loredo y Valderrama, an ordinary man with an extraordinary capacity for candor. Finding it impossible to accept the existence of deceit, fraud, and the numerous hypocrisies that are encountered in every walk of life, Dominico feels that it is his moral obligation to denounce wrongdoing in any form, regardless of the consequences. When a less-than-virtuous secretary asks him why he has meddled in her affairs and caused her to be fired, he gives what to him is sufficient reason:

DOMINICO. I was not born to watch anything that is done improperly, as if it had nothing to do with me. I straighten pictures on walls, I get out of the car to remove rocks from the highways, and I pick up paper that other people have thrown on the ground and put it in a wastebasket. I caution pedestrians who are crossing the street where they aren't supposed to . . . I have a very strict sense of obligation and I live up to it, come what may. For me, fraud, lying, and cheating are things that should be eliminated. And I've dedicated myself to that goal.[54]

Dominico has been hired by a company with the pointedly satirical title of SAPPLIS (*Sociedad Anónima de Productos Plásticos y Sintéticos*) ("Plastics and Synthetics, Inc.") through the personal intervention of the "Minister of Supplies." He immediately tells his employer, Don Gregorio, that the salaries of the cleaning women should be increased; and when he discovers that the director's secretary-mistress (Matilde) also has a liaison with a second lover, he exposes her duplicity. Dominico is attracted to one of the cleaning women (Rosa) and spends a night with her. The following morning she is amazed when he insists that he wants to do the "right thing" and marry her. Her own comments reveal a more resigned outlook on life:

ROSA. My aunt Roseada—the one they named me Rosa for—used to say, to get the bad taste out of her mouth, that life was like a trip that we all begin starched and scrubbed. But along the way we quickly get dirtied with grime and dust. You've been traveling for quite a while now, my dear, and you're as clean as the day your mother first soaped you down.[55]

Dominico finds his supreme cause when he discovers the financial double-dealings in the bookkeeping department of SAPPLIS. He threatens to expose the company if Don Gregorio does not make amends within a stated period of time. Recognizing that Dominico is dead serious, Gregorio starts an investigation of his office worker's past with the aid of a wily character named Ginés. They find out that "The Innocent Soul" had been released from the army and placed on inactive status because of his candor. While on guard duty he had come upon a homosexual *ménage à trois* involving two recruits and the son of the Minister of Supplies (which explains why the minister had interceded for Dominico at SAPPLIS). With this information in hand, Ginés plots to destroy Dominico's credibility. When the unsuspecting man goes to see a film at the Cine Miami, he is followed by a youth (Tony) and a hired witness. Tony sits beside him and after a moment accuses him of a homosexual overture. The witness, of course, comes forward to substantiate the accusation, and Dominico is taken away by the police.

In a scene depicting a meeting of the stockholders of SAPPLIS, Calvo-Sotelo achieves a devastating satire of this ritual function of big business. Dominico attempts to denounce the company to the indifferent assembly, and a voice from the balcony calls out "Faggot!" When the excitement causes Don Gregorio to collapse from a heart attack, the chorus mockingly begins to chant:

Oh, myocardic infarction, guillotine of the rich,
Faithful guest of the Stock Exchange. . . .lightning without thunder.[56]

In the play's final scene, Dominico is standing on a subway platform, ready to throw himself in front of a train. Rosa appears and urges him to keep on living, to come home with her. Whether because of censorship demands or a personal reluctance to permit Dominico to commit the sin of suicide (a self-destruction that had seemed inevitable), Calvo-Sotelo softened his ending by allowing his protagonist to find salvation of sorts. Consequently, what might have been the most searing moment in the playwright's entire theater is lost. At the time of the premiere of *The Innocent Soul*, some critics called the play a tragicomedy;[57] but, in truth, the tragic dimension is seriously diminished at the end. Perhaps the work can better be described as a dark, satirical comedy.

In the *autocrítica* for the work, the author explained his theme as "the conflict between individual purity, rare as a hothouse flower, and the impurity of the human jungle that stifles and corrupts."[58] Unfortunately, Dominico's candor—his major demonstration of "purity"—appears at times more like stubborness than innate goodness. As a character he never approaches the grandeur or the nobility that have elevated single-mindedness, nonconformity, and obsessions in the literature of the past. He is, to be sure, an antihero, intentionally portrayed as the "nobody" of Western society in the mid-twentieth century, an insignificant man with no claim to accomplishment other than the peculiar mischief that stems from his absolute honesty. Furthermore, Calvo-Sotelo's character is a supremely dull man, whose taste is pedestrian (he reads old issues of magazines and finds distraction in war films, westerns, and soap operas) and whose life is humdrum (at age forty-nine, romantic love has passed him by).

The impact of the author's writing is strongest in the scene which satirizes the corruption of big business and in the truly brutal scene in the motion picture theater in which the false accusations of homosexuality are made against Dominico. However, throughout the work, the dialogue and passages for the chorus are skillfully integrated and remarkably forceful. In spite of the reservations about the central character and his ultimate destiny, *The Innocent Soul* is never less than a vivid and disturbing dramatic creation.

Other Calvo-Sotelo plays of the past decade include *La condesa*

Laurel (Countess Laurel, 1964), which treats the theme of loneliness; *El poder* (Power, 1965), a serious drama set in the Renaissance; *El baño de las ninfas* (The Nymphs' Bath, 1966), dealing with a republican leader who lives disguised as a nun in a convent under the protection of the religious community so that he can avoid capture by the Nationalists; *La amante* (The Lover, 1968), a bittersweet drama about the conflicts of illusions and reality; and *El alfil* (The Bishop, 1970), one of the playwright's more melodramatic works.

Calvo-Sotelo's vast dramatic output encompasses both essays into the trivial and ambitious considerations of human dilemmas. In his comedies he has not demonstrated an unmistakable personal style nor has he created a work of the polish or insight that we find in the best comic creations of López Rubio or Mihura. Most of his serious dramas are flawed. Ruiz Ramón has noted two basic obstacles to the success and universality of some of the playwright's most acclaimed efforts: a tendency to go overboard and include what is not necessary dramatically and aesthetically, leading to excessive melodrama, and the urge to treat the theme that is most timely—if not the most enduring.[59] His serious theater lacks the visionary quality that illuminates the dramas of Buero-Vallejo, and his conservative social philosophy excludes the commitment to social change that has inspired Sastre, Olmo, and other younger Spanish dramatists. Nevertheless, works of the caliber of *The Trial of Archbishop Carranza*, *The Innocent One*, and *The Wall* represent a not insubstantial contribution to the theater of the postwar period.

IV *José María Pemán*

José María Pemán y Pemartín is one of Spain's senior dramatists and the only active contributor to the contemporary theater whose career reached a peak prior to the establishment of the nationalist regime in 1939. Born in Cadiz in 1898, Pemán became thoroughly imbued with the culture of Andalusia in his early years. Later, as a student, he lived both in Seville and in Madrid, where he earned a doctorate in law. He published his first collection of poetry in 1923, and a decade later he achieved renown as a playwright with his historical drama in verse *El divino impaciente* (The Impatient Saint) which dealt with the life

of St. Francis Xavier, the sixteenth-century Jesuit missionary. As
president of the conservative group "Acción Española" during the
period of the republic, he was also recognized as an articulate
spokesman for traditional Spanish values. In 1936 he was elected
to membership in the Royal Spanish Academy of Letters but did
not take his seat until the end of the civil war. He also served as
director of the academy for several years.

Pemán's body of dramatic works, dating from the late 1920's to
the present decade, is substantial. And since he has also
cultivated extensively the genres of poetry and the essay, it is
clear that his has been a life seriously dedicated to literary
creativity. Like a number of other twentieth-century Spanish
dramatists, his plays reveal a variety of thematic material and
include both ambitious serious dramas of several types and
comedies. Throughout his long and virtually uninterrupted career
he has demonstrated a consistent adherence to established
theatrical forms and an unconcealed admiration for the classical
writers of the past, particularly the eighteenth-century Spanish
master of comedy, Leandro Fernández de Moratín. Pemán's
historical dramas, which follow paths similar to those of Eduardo
Marquina, look to the past of both Spain and Europe, as the titles
indicate: Cisneros (1935), Metternich (1942), La destrucción de
Sagunto (The Destruction of Saguntum, 1954), etc. Other works
by Pemán are modern treatments, either in verse or prose, of
classical themes, such as Antígona (1946), Electra (1949), Epido
(Oedipus, 1953), and Tyestes (1955). In some instances he follows
the model of Giraudoux in instilling his modernizations with
contemporaneity of speech and ironic comment or humor.[60] In
the case of his Oedipus, he attempts to create a stately but
suspenseful poetic version of an especially familiar legend that
will capture and hold the attention of present-day audiences.

Still another type of theater that the author favors is the
moralistic drama placed more or less in a contemporary setting
and dealing with matters of faith and conscience interpreted in
terms of his own devout Catholicism. Although Pemán's lighter
comic works do not reveal any strong personal style or innovative
tendencies, his most successful and perhaps most enduring
theatrical piece of the postwar period is the brisk and witty
comedy Las tres etcéteras de don Simón (Don Simón's Three
Etceteras, 1958). On October 15, 1949—one day after the

memorable premiere of Buero-Vallejo's *Story of a Stair-way*—the first of Pemán's three offerings of the 1949-50 theatrical season opened in Madrid. *El viejo y las niñas* (The Old Man and His Lasses) merits consideration because it is illustrative of a type of bittersweet comedy that has been produced by a number of twentieth-century playwrights—occasionally with genuinely artistic results. Pemán's play—a curious blend of humor, mystery, eccentricity, anguish, and tenderness—is not one of the more successful of its genre even though it provides considerable evidence of the author's serious intent and his understanding of the theatrical possibilities of the varied scenes.

The comedy is set in the playwright's native city of Cadiz at the time of the yearly Corpus Christi festival, when crowds of outsiders are arriving. The opening act takes place in the lobby of a picturesque but decidedly second-class hotel. Various characters are introduced: a conceited young poet; an affable middle-aged doctor named Fermín; a guide who speaks with the Andalusian accent that has been exploited so frequently in Spanish comedy; two town gossips; and, finally, an eccentric elderly man (Don Lucas) who arrives in the company of two attractive women (Lina, a girl in her late teens, and Adela, who is more mature). Even after the conspicious appearance of the trio, the direction the play is taking is not completely clear. Questions are asked: Are Adela and Lina sisters: Mother and daughter? Is Adela married to Don Lucas? Fermín is attracted to Adela but is unsure of her status. The mystery extends to the very end of the play where it is revealed that Lina, who is Adela's illegitimate daughter, is also Don Lucas's wife and that she is expecting a child.

The title of the comedy was inspired by Moratín's *El viejo y la niña* (The Old Man and the Lass), and Pemán's idea was to show that there is more than one possible outcome to the love of an aging man for a young girl, that a May-December romance can be fruitful and not result in the humiliation of the man. But the author has drawn on more sources than Moratín. There are touches of Benavente in the piquant but genteel dialogue, and of the Quintero brothers in the calculated use of Andalusian speech and mores. Don Lucas and his companions live in a special world that they have created to cope with the negative attitudes of society, and in their somewhat eccentric pastimes and schemes to mystify they resemble some of the more extravagantly peculiar characters that Jardiel Poncela, Mihura, and López Rubio have manipulated so adroitly.

Several of Pemán's works of the 1950's fall under the general heading of moralistic drama. *Callados como los muertos* (Silent as the Dead, 1952) presents an improbable situation in which a nationalist diplomat, married to a woman who had favored the republic, becomes the protector of his wife's former lover. Ultimately, the play makes little or no genuine political comment but rather brings the problem to a level of personal conscience. *En las manos del hijo* (In the Hands of the Son, 1953) is another example of this type of emotion-laden drama that contributed to Pemán's reputation in Spain as a spokesman for traditional religious and ethical values. But it is a play that does not travel well beyond the Pyrenees. The plot is relatively straightforward: José Luis, the son of an overprotective mother (Mercedes) becomes a priest and must accept the "confession" of the mother that she had had a relationship with a family friend and aide prior to the death of her invalid husband. Chalo, the older "prodigal son" returns from America with a mistress (Alma) who poses as his wife. His hedonistic views come into direct conflict with the Catholicism of the mother and the almost saintly manner of José Luis. In the final act, the action becomes diffuse and the focus moves from the struggle between Mercedes's faith and her desire for personal fulfillment to the redemption of Chalo's mistress and the mother's hope for the ultimate return of the son who has strayed. Admittedly, the drama has flashes of psychological insight and provides a highly theatrical role for a mature actress, but the old-fashioned rhetoric of the emotionally-charged confrontation scenes comes, for an audience of our own period, perilously close to the ridiculous at times.

El viento sobre la tierra (The Wind Over the Earth, 1957) is a political drama with its political views implied rather than specified. The playwright shows himself to be firmly on the side of tradition, stability, and continuity while favoring a strong sense of personal patriotism; youth is pictured as rebellious and susceptible to evil influences. But in essence the work is a family drama of divided interests rather than any clear ideological statement. The plot deals with the return to power of a respected leader (Victorio) who has been exiled by a successful revolution.

His own son (Pablo) had supported the revolt, and a close associate (Patricio) goes over to the "enemy." When the counter-revolution is underway, Pablo sacrifices his life to prevent the slaughter of his father and other prisoners. Emma, Victorio's wife, personally assassinates the traitor Patricio. Rarely has a serious contemporary drama seemed so out of touch with reality or so antiquated in its language and style. It reaches its dramatic nadir in a scene in which Victorio, to show his paternal love, kisses his son and immediately strikes him in the face to express his contempt for his revolutionary activities. And when Emma describes the encounter that resulted in her killing Patricio, we find dialogue that might have been conceived by Sardou. Whereas *Silent as the Dead* and *In the Hands of the Son* have moments of effective drama in spite of their dated sentiments, *The Wind Over the Earth*, with its blatant histrionics and its pretentious dialogue, is a total miscalculation.

Fortunately, in 1958, Pemán picked up his Moratinian inspiration once more and produced a small but admirable example of comic art. Even the less respectful critics have acknowledged the aesthetic values of *Las tres etcéteras de don Simón* (Don Simón's Three Etceteras). William Giuliano, in a detailed analysis, describes the play as "a farce of much wit with sufficient psychological depth to merit a place among the best works of its class in the contemporary theater."[61] The comedy is, indeed, a laughter-provoking delight, filled with sharp and felicitous dialogue which touches satirically on well-known Spanish foibles and reveals a keen understanding of the emotional frailties of both men and women.

The action of *Don Simón's Three Etceteras* is set in the past (1810) during the period of Napoleonic rule in Spain in a village called La Fernandina (Fernando was the deposed king). A message arrives for the mayor (Lucas) announcing the arrival of the regional governor (Don Simón) and requesting appropriate lodgings, good chocolate, special wines, first-rate coffee, etcetera, etcetera, etcetera. Since the expression "etcetera" is not in the mayor's vocabulary, he interprets the instructions to mean that Don Simón expects three females for his personal attention. There is only one prostitute in town—the quick-witted Georgina Mendicutia, commonly known as Marifácil—and no one knows how to produce additional "etceteras" without compromising the honor of a daughter or wife. But through their own plotting, two other young women (Rosina and Fernanda) do end up in the governor's quarters. Rosina is in love with the rebel soldier "El Mastín de Sabañigos." By gaining Don Simón's affection and respect, she is reunited with her impetuous lover. Fernanda also resolves her personal amorous difficulties through her association with the governor. But it is Marifácil who stands out in the play with her special earthy wisdom and understanding.

Pemán has not shown a disinclination to renewal of his dramatic impulse or an indifference to the changing patterns of society. But, expectedly, his attitudes toward these changes remain those of the traditionalist and conservative. In 1963 he wrote *Los monos gritan al amanecer* (Monkeys Cry Out at Dawn),[62] a compact little drama about the amoral lives of a group of cynical and disenchanted young people on the edge of the artistic world. One couple commit suicide with cyanide capsules after publicly announcing their intention. The happiness of Elena, the principal female character, is threatened because she cannot shed the guilt of her past. (Her most specific indiscretion had been to pose in the nude for a callous sculptor.) The only character with true nobility is the mother of the young man who loves Elena. The playwright's attempt to create believable dialogue for the generation of the 1960's is not always successful, and he fails to suggest very strongly that in the sterile existences of his characters there are determining factors beyond their rejection of strict religious and ethical values.

Tres testigos (Three Witnesses, 1970) is a serious drama that invites a reevaluation of Pemán's theater. It is not only one of his most carefully constructed plays, it is also refreshingly free of the melodramatic excesses that too frequently distort the honest intent of his work. Pemán has drawn on his vast knowledge of classical and modern theater for the composition of *Three Witnesses* (the basic situation having been suggested by a short English novel by Walker Macken). But the result is original and personal. It is a moralistic drama, to be sure, which reflects the author's familiar ethical stance; it is also an authentic modern tragedy.

The entire action of the play takes place in an isolated mountain lodge where the three principal characters—Robi, Mari Ana, and Trinidad—and a judge (who confides to the audience that he may simply be called "Conscience") have assembled for a hearing. Robi, a man of fifty-nine, has brought up his motherless daughter, Mari Ana, with great care, keeping her safe and remote from the temptations of the world below. (The physical location of the lodge suggests a certain spiritual elevation.) Ana, the half-Danish and half-Spanish mother, had died shortly after the girl's birth. Robi had met and fallen in love with her while she had been hitchhiking through Spain. In reality Robi had never touched Ana, and Mari Ana's father had been an anonymous man that Ana had encountered while in an alcoholic stupor. Nevertheless, Robi decides to marry the young woman and to honor her dying request for him to care for "their" child. As the years pass, his love becomes less than strictly paternal. Since the child is not his own, his feelings are incestuous only in terms of the relationship that he has honorably assumed. Robi begins to accept guests at the lodge—but only women. Through a misinterpretation of his gender due to an ambiguous name (Trinidad), a young Cuban botanist is also received as a paying guest. He and Mari Ana fall in love. Robi considers him a threat and gives forceful indications of his opposition to any ideas of marriage. However, he draws back just short of overt violence. Trinidad refuses to be intimidated and takes the girl away.

Each character relates his story to the judge, and events of the past, including scenes in which the mother appears, are reenacted. Robi does not destroy the image that Mari Ana has of her mother by revealing to her or to her husband the true circumstances of her birth. Sadly, their communication becomes limited to near ritualistic letters that both writer and recipient recognize as being false; and conversation on the occasions when they are together is of the kind that men use so frequently merely to break the silences. At the end of the play, the three characters ask questions that perplex them and which will not be answered:

TRINIDAD. Was it better not to know without demanding a greater clarification?
MARI ANA. Should I have cried out? . . . Not returned without understanding?
ROBI. Was it all a punishment for Ana's one night of madness?
TRINIDAD. What superior force plays with us?
ROBI. And punishes by condemning us to the ultimate loneliness?

MARI ANA. Why can't we leap over the moat of silence that surrounds us?
TRINIDAD. We are not three witnesses, your honor . . . but three islands without bridges.
ROBI. Three parts of truth.
MARI ANA. Three pieces of silence.[63]

The judge then renounces his right to decide:

JUDGE. *(To the audience.)* Perhaps I should swear you in as a jury for this decision. You judge those questions for yourselves. Did one of them do the right thing? The other? Or still another? What is the truth of each of them? No one will dare to pass sentence . . . *(He slowly takes the papers from the table and tears them up.)* Neither shall I. The final judgment on such matters . . . exceeds the understanding of men. The final word must be left to God.[64]

Three Witnesses bears some superficial resemblances to Ruiz Iriarte's *Story of a Deceit,* which had been seen in 1969. Both plays have characters who represent conscience and function as a type of counsel, and the past is reenacted in order to present different views of reality. However, in actual substance the two are quite different. The earlier work is more theatrical and does not invite so pointedly the participation of the audience in the "hearing," while Pemán's drama is more consciously intellectual and moralistic in those aspects dealing with incest linked to moral obligation rather than blood ties. The Phaedra-Hippolytus legend most certainly influenced the conception of the play (just as Racine's *Phèdre* provided a title and seed of inspiration for López Rubio's equally restrained drama of conscience, *Our Hands are Innocent,* in 1958). When considering the question of incest in the Spanish theater, Benavente's *La malquerida* inevitably comes to mind, though that work is vastly different from Pemán's drama in its realization.

Pemán's failure to allow his action to follow what might seem an inevitable course toward a violent ending has been criticized. In a colloquium on the work in which a number of prominent theatrical figures participated, Luis Núñez Ladevece, the drama critic for *Nuevo Diario,* remarked: "*Three Witnesses* is perhaps the best theatrical work that has come from the pen of José María Pemán. It is a pity, from my point of view, that he has not provided a denouement that carried the action to its ultimate consequences . . . fulfilling the tragedy. It would have been more theatrical, more forceful."[65] But Alfredo Marquerie notes in the same discussion that the ending is totally *"pemaniano"* and in accord with the author's custom of "insinuating without consummating."[66] For Pemán the tragedy is the silence that has been forced upon the characters by Robi's refusal to justify his own emotions by destroying the memory of a woman he had loved—a view that is in keeping with the playwright's enduring concern for a guiding sense of moral direction and obligation in human lives.

Now well into his seventies, Pemán continues to be active on the theatrical scene in Madrid. Perhaps it is some indication of a certain youthfulness of spirit that his most recent undertaking (with José Luis Martín Descalzo) has been a Spanish adaptation of the American musical play *Godspell*.

V *Juan Ignacio Luca de Tena*

Juan Ignacio Luca de Tena (b. 1897) is another senior playwright of notable prolificness whose career has spanned some four decades; his total body of dramatic writing includes more than forty titles. A member of the publishing dynasty that founded Madrid's leading daily, *A B C*, in 1905, and the popular weekly magazine *Blanco y Negro*, Luca de Tena has held the directorship of both publications on occasion. In 1923, at the age of twenty-six, he became a deputy to the Spanish Cortes from his native city of Seville. After the establishment of the nationalist government in 1939, he served for four years as Ambassador to Chile. In 1944 he was elected to membership in the Royal Spanish Academy of Letters. Given the variety of his time-consuming activities, it is remarkable that he has been able to devote himself so assiduously to the creation of new works for the stage.

Like Pemán and Calvo-Sotelo, Luca de Tena has varied his dramatic product throughout his career, alternating plays which reveal serious intellectual pretensions with lighter pieces in the comic or mystery vein. Consequently, it is difficult to trace a direct line of development in his work or to identify a personal element that is consistently present. However, the influence of

Pirandello is notably present in several of his works of the 1930's and 1940's. One of his most discussed offerings of the postwar period was the "historical" melodrama *El cóndor sin alas* (The Wingless Condor), which was performed in 1951. The work was written to order for a drama competition in which all the entries had a single thesis to prove: "that the difference in cultural level between individuals excludes the possibility of close understanding between the social classes." Literally hundreds of plays were submitted on this decidedly specialized and questionable proposition, and considerable controversy was stirred up over the selection of the panel of judges and the awarding of the prize. Luca de Tena called his work a "historical tryptich," and, not surprisingly, its political content was meager. In Torrente Ballester's opinion, *The Wingless Condor* is a failure. In fact, the outspoken critic suggests that the author succeeded in demonstrating exactly the opposite of what he set out to do in his story of upward movement and marriage in Spanish social strata.[67]

Luca de Tena has also produced his share of slick entertainment of the type of *Don José, Pepe y Pepito* (Joseph, Joe and Joey), which won for him the National Prize for Drama in 1952—even though the comedy is utterly ephemeral. In this inoffensive piece the major characters are educated, articulate people who show their sophistication by speaking wittily or wisely and by dropping names (from Echegaray to Elizabeth Taylor). The arrows of love penetrate their cool facades and complications arise. Three generations—grandfather, father, and son—become infatuated with an extraordinary female executive from the United States—Francis Grey,[68] who had been conveniently born in Madrid to ensure the fluency of her Spanish. There is also the stereotype of the indignant rival who demonstrates a command of the language of international bitchiness. Father and son are momentarily alienated, but Francis decides to make a sacrifice and leave Spain. Reconciliation is prompt, and a happy ending is implied. All of the elements are put together with precision and a fine sense of theater to produce a comic diversion that in its day would have passed muster on Broadway or in the West End.

Luca de Tena's two historical dramas on the ill-fated Alfonso XII cannot be ignored. *¿Dónde vas, Alfonso XII?* (Where Now, Alfonso XII?, 1957) and *¿Dónde vas, triste de ti?* (Where Now,

Sad Friend?, 1959) represent the playwright's most successful efforts of the 1950's and show his flair for creating effective theatrical moments if not totally memorable dramas. The titles for the two plays are taken from a popular ballad recalling the king's personal tragedy which circulated in Spain after the death of his first wife. Lines from the song provide a moving ending for *Where Now, Alfonso XII?* and are effectively integrated into the early scenes of the play that followed. The first of the two works covers the period 1870-1878 and is mainly concerned with the romance of the young Alfonso and María de las Mercedes, the events leading to the restoration of the Bourbon dynasty in Spain, and the tragic death of the young queen. Direct quotations from letters and documented statements of the royal family and of political leaders lend authenticity to the dialogue and indicate careful research on the part of the author. The sequel, *Where Now, Sad Friend?*, begins one year after the death of Mercedes and ends with the death of Alfonso and the beginning of the regency of his second wife, Queen María Cristina (some months before the birth of the king's heir, Alfonso XIII). If the second play has less direct appeal than the first, it is because it attempts to incorporate too great a range of historical events into the action and lacks the bittersweet story of a king who married for love. It is hardly surprising that the drama is most affecting when the dialogue touches on events that are treated in the earlier play.

Luca de Tena's political sentiments are strongly monarchist, and he presents Alfonso and the later regent, María Cristina, in a highly favorable light. The words of the young prince as he explains his role to his reactionary and blundering mother sound strikingly like the contemporary justifications for the monarchy that have been set forth in the Spanish press: ". . . the great advantage of monarchies can be found in their ability to adjust to changing times and to all situations, because their historical mission and their continuity are above situations and times."[69] But Luca de Tena's "Alfonso" plays should not be dismissed simply because they represent a nostalgic, romanticized view of history and support an ideological stance that is given small credit in most Western countries. Both are respectable dramas of considerable dignity, with certain scenes of undeniable theatrical impact. Perhaps the principal limitation of the two plays is the result of the author's failure to give a more conspicuous role to the people of Spain whose destiny was so drastically affected by the confused political events of the late nineteenth century.

The playwright's major success of the past decade was a revival in 1966 of ¿Quien soy yo? (Who Am I?), a work that had first been staged in 1935. After a run of some 700 performances, it was followed in 1969 by the production of a sequel, Yo soy Brandel (I am Brandel). Who Am I? proclaims its Pirandellian affiliations as strongly as Calvo-Sotelo's The Godless City. The complex plot deals with the employment of a double (Brandel) for a politician (Colomer) who is too sincere and introverted to rise to the highest position of power. As one character expresses it, "I consider Colomer an exceptional man. For me he has only one defect: the fact that he has no defect at all." Brandel possesses the very quality that Colomer needs to further his career: a charismatic manner that seduces the public. Once the stand-in assumes his "role" his influence grows and because of his personal warmth he even gains the love of Claudina, the woman Colomer plans to marry. But he becomes more of a threat than a help, and in the final act Colomer attempts to eliminate his rival. As the two men struggle, the audience sees them only in silhouette; a shot is fired and one of the men escapes as the house is consumed in flames. Although the question, "Who am I?", is not answered, there are implications that it is Brandel who survived. In the sequel, Brandel must become Colomer, but in time he reveals his true identity to Claudina and renounces his "role."

One may conclude that the second play was unnecessary and that it has the effect of destroying some of the dramatic validity of Who Am I?. The playwright has obviously found models for his first play in works of both Pirandello and Unamuno,[70] but the final result is a pure suspense-mystery drama in which the identity question lacks the element of unresolvable enigma that is fundamental to Pirandello's Così è (se vi pare), or the metaphysical concern that underlies the theater of Unamuno. I am Brandel prolongs the mystery and provides an interesting development of Brandel's predicament after he has killed Colomer, but such a continuation, one may assume, would have been unthinkable for either Pirandello or Unamuno.

In recent years several new works and adaptations by Luca de Tena have been seen on the Madrid stage, but none has created nearly the interest generated by the pair of plays that had been written during the period of the republic.

VI *Edgar Neville*

Edgar Neville's contributions to the contemporary Spanish stage seem modest and unpretentious when compared with the prolific output of Pemán, Luca de Tena, or Calvo-Sotelo. However, in addition to his dozen or so theatrical titles, he also wrote more than twenty-five scenarios for motion pictures, countless short stories, and a novel. Born into Spanish nobility in 1899, Neville bore the title of Count of Berlanga de Duero. As a young man he studied law in Granada, where he came to know García Lorca, and later entered the diplomatic corps. Like López Rubio, Jardiel Poncela, and Tono, he spent a period in Hollywood after the introduction of sound preparing Spanish versions of American films (dubbing had not yet been perfected) and advising on production. An interesting memento of his three years in California is his appearance as a policeman in the Chaplin film *City Lights*. A man both affable and sardonic, Neville was an associate of many theatrical personalities of the century. Cocteau, Chaplin, Mihura, López Rubio, and Marcel Achard, to name a few. Victor Ruiz Iriarte has written a splendid tribute to his late friend,[71] bringing to light some of the paradoxical qualities of a complex individual who bought his clothes at the finest shops of London, Madrid, and Paris and wore them with the carelessness of a *fin de siècle* bohemian. He was a writer who demonstrated exceptional verbal grace and poetic insight on occasion and yet was capable of casually dictating lines of dialogue to a secretary. Neville's very early play, *La vía láctea (The Milky Way)* opened in 1917 but was quickly closed by the police. After his first important work, *Margarita y los hombres* (Margarita and Men), was staged in Madrid in 1934, the author did not return to playwriting until the 1950's. In 1952 the production of *El Baile* (The Dance) brought him new acclaim. This sentimental but tastefully written comedy became one of the great popular successes of the modern Spanish theater. A series of light but individualistic comic works and several adaptations of foreign plays followed over the next decade. In 1968, Neville died at the age of sixty-nine.

The Dance is constructed of the most fragile materials, and with less skillful craftsmanship it could have been an embarrassment. The protagonist, Adela, has been courted by two friends, Julián and Pedro, who have two dominant passions: their love for the same woman and the hobby of collecting specimens of rare insects. Pedro marries Adela while Julián is away in America; but on the friend's return they find a solution to the problem by incorporating him into their household. At the end of the first act the trio remains happily at home drinking champagne instead of attending a costume ball. To the delight of both men, Adela announces that she is pregnant. In the second act the mood shifts from the lighthearted and whimsical to the sad. It is now 1925; the child has grown up and is living in the United States. Adela expresses a desire to travel and to have a taste of adventure before old age makes it impossible. A doctor's report brings the stunning information that Adela has only three months to live. The friends abandon their insect hobby to devote their energies to making the final days of their beloved magnificent. Adela discovers the doctor's letter but she hides her knowledge of her true condition from the men who love her. The final act takes place in the present. Adela's granddaughter Adelita (played by the same actress) is visiting her "grandfathers." She begins to fill the void that had existed since Adela's death. Although her plans had been to rejoin her mother in America, she elects to remain with the elderly men and devote a period of her life to their happiness. Instead of rushing off to a dance she had planned to attend, she remains in the apartment drinking champagne and dancing with Pedro and Julián. The scene is a replica of the act 1 finale, and Adelita unknowingly repeats the very words that her grandmother had spoken at the end of act 1: "Thank you for your love, thank you."

The world of *The Dance* is a special one that can occur only in the theater. That such a bittersweet and improbable love triangle could prove so credible and affecting is a tribute to the author's special awareness of the line that divides genuine sentiment from bathos. The ending of the comedy is similar to that of Ruiz Iriarte's *The Six-Horse Landau* (in which a young person temporarily renounces the world to take the place of an elderly woman who knows she is dying). Both plays are redeemed by a sense of poetic reality that makes unorthodox situations dramatically purposeful. *The Dance* remains modest in every respect except one: the role of Adela-Adelita requires a virtuoso actress capable of expressing shifts of emotion from lightheartedness to an awareness of imminent tragedy. Apparently Conchita Montes realized to the fullest the potential of the part.

Adelita (1955), the sequel to *The Dance*, carries forward the relationship of the young girl and her elderly guardians. Julián dies at the end of act 1, and at the end of the play the same "Gray Lady" who lured him to the other world comes for Pedro. However, the comic and the pathetic do not blend so successfully in this work, and its dramatic interest is not consistent. *Veinte añitos* (Twenty Slight Years, 1954) is a comical treatment of the Faust theme, complete with a modern "Vice-Devil" who prefers negotiable items to human souls. The twist in the plot results from the rejuvenation of both a middle-aged man and his wife. The wife eventually rejects the love of a young admirer to return to the existence to which she has grown accustomed with her husband. Neville demonstrates that age is not merely physical change, that we are products of our time and that to be rejuvenated in body is not sufficient for becoming a part of a younger generation. The play grows in depth after its trivial beginning but ends with a conventionally happy denouement of no particular dramatic distinction.

Neville must be adjudged a successful playwright, for he understood the nature of his own gifts and did not attempt to write beyond the limits of the skills he possessed. He also avoided a facile formula that could have made him a more prolific dramatist. Other plays of his late career are *Prohibido en otoño* (Forbidden in Autumn, 1957), *Alta fidelidad* (High Fidelity, 1957), *La vida en un hilo* (Life on a Thread, 1959)—first a film scenario, then a stage play, and finally a musical comedy in the 1960's—and *La extraña noche de boda* (The Strange Wedding Night, 1963). Though none of these comedies can be considered truly important examples of Spanish dramatic literature, by the same token none is lacking in taste and a refined sense of theatrical style.

CHAPTER 3

New Writers of The Post-Civil War Theater

I Víctor Ruiz Iriarte

VICTOR Ruiz Iriarte (b. 1912) was the first new dramatic writer of promise to appear on the theatrical scene during the years immediately following the end of the Spanish civil war. As a child he had eagerly read the old collections of plays that he had found in his home, and by the age of fifteen he had begun to write his own dramas. The war years were a period in which the aspiring young dramatist had little opportunity to develop his talents or find guidance; but in the early 1940's he participated in the literary *tertulias* at the Café Gijón and was aware of whatever creative activities were being undertaken in those difficult years. (Camilo José Cela also frequented the Gijón and dedicated his first novel, *The Family of Pascual Duarte*, to his friend Ruiz Iriarte.) The playwright reports that after the performance of his one-act comedy *Un día en la gloria* (A Day in Heaven) in 1943 he tore up "a respectable pile" of unpublished efforts and started anew.[1] The production of his first full-length play, *El puente de los suicidas* (Suicide Bridge) in 1944 brought him critical attention and comparisons of his work with that of Casona. But it was not until the premiere of *El aprendiz de amante* (The Apprentice Lover) in 1947 that he enjoyed genuine public approval. He began to write with a new confidence, and all of his plays of the early 1950's show the stamp of a skillful professional. Also, we see the emergence of a personal aesthetic of dramatic composition that sets Ruiz Iriarte apart from a number of other contemporary writers whose borrowed techniques failed to evidence any pronounced individual development.

With *El landó de seis caballos* (The Six-Horse Landau) in 1950, the playwright's reputation was firmly established. This appealing "sad comedy" lies somewhere between certain plays of

Marcel Achard and those of Jean Anouilh in its Pirandellian inspiration and its presentation of life theatricalized. Like so many serious comedies of the postwar period, *The Six-Horse Landau* is set in a place remote from the realities and conflicts of a mechanized society. Three young women of varied personalities (Margarita, Rosita, and Isabel), a young man named Florencio, and a jazz musician called Bobby receive letters suggesting that they will find the possibility of happiness if they come to a villa on the outskirts of Avila. The notes are signed by a duke, but the real author turns out to be a doctor who knows them all. The guests find themselves transported to a strange, nostalgic world that time and change seem to have ignored, where a group of old people (Doña Adelita, Chapete, Simón, and Pedro) joyfully engage in rides through the park dressed in turn-of-the-century attire and singing old ballads. However, their "coach" consists of chairs and a sofa, and the "rides" are purely imaginary. How each of the young people reacts to this bizarre charade is determined by his or her susceptibility to the more poetic aspects of the situation. Isabel, the most sentimental of the girls, finds some meaning in what appears to the others to be extreme eccentricity at best; and she begins to convert Florencio to her way of thinking.

In the second act, Doña Adelita discloses the true history of the six-horse landau in a speech that in no way conceals its antecedent in Pirandello's *Enrico IV*. She explains to Isabel and Florencio that she herself has only a short time to live and that someone must continue the "rides" for the sake of the survivors—Chapete in particular:

ADELITA. The only one who is really mad is Chapete. He went insane many years ago when he was driving the duke to the races in that beautiful landau. A coach that was all black and glistening! The horses had silver buckles! . . . (*She smiles.*) Chapete was a handsome lad! He handled the horses with a flair. I had very dark hair and laughing eyes. We loved each other so much. We were going to be married soon. But then the accident happened.
ISABEL. What accident?
ADELITA. One morning . . . a horse reared up and Chapete couldn't control him. The horses ran wild with the coach. Nothing happened to the duke but Chapete received a blow on the head. From that day . . . Chapete has lived in a dream world. In his imagination he's still

driving the duke's handsome landau. But in his mind he has turned it into the most marvelous of all carriages; now it has six horses . . . Since the duke brought us to Las Colinas in 1910, I've seen to it that time and reality halt at the door of this house. . . . We play a game. For dreams are nothing more than a game. We have made life a game too.[2]

Although Chapete's madness results from an accident very much like the one that stopped time for Pirandello's Enrico, Ruiz Iriarte's characters are obviously living a more sentimental or poeticized play-within-a-play. It is worthy of note that the playwright has introduced into this work a concept that is fundamental to many of his subsequent plays: that we continually turn life into a game or "play" that can either provide a route to a more authentic existence or be fraught with dangers.

At the end of *The Six-Horse Landau*, as the other guests return to their conventional reality, Isabel—over the protests of Florencio—decides to remain and devote a period of her life to prolonging the illusion of the aging men after Adelita dies. Florencio warns her:

FLORENCIO. . . . Real life is far from here. In this house there are only imagination, dreams, lies. Those four old people are only ghosts of themselves. It would be madness to stay here to share the manias of people who've gone insane from loneliness.
ISABEL. I'm staying. The invitation that may have seemed a joke for the rest of you has given me a mission.[3]

Then Florencio remains with her for a trial "ride," and they join the "insane" group to sing the nostalgic ballad of the sad love of Alfonso XII for Mercedes:

Where now, Alfonso Twelfth?
Where now, sad friend?
"I go in search of Mercedes,
For I found her not
When day was at end."[4]

Whether we choose to use the much abused label *"teatro de evasión"* or seek a more adequate description for such a work of poetized reality, *The Six-Horse Landau* should not be confused with the fabricated and trivial comedies that can be dismissed as escapist entertainment. It is not a conventionally happy-ending play by any means but rather it provokes a serious consideration of the essential, but sometimes dangerous, role of illusion in human survival—albeit from a sentimental viewpoint.

On December 8, 1950, *El gran minué* (The Grand Minuet) opened in Madrid. Called by the author a "farce-ballet" and set in an imaginary eighteenth-century court (that does seem decidedly French), the play recalls at times Benavente's *Los intereses creados* (The Bonds of Interest). An opening prologue spoken by the ingenue (Diana) tells the audience to prepare itself for a *juego* ("game") in which actors in makeup will conspire and in which the mischief of words will make harmony with the violins of the orchestra. There are similarities both to the prologue of Benavente's comedy and to Crispín's later speech in which he states that life is a party where music serves to cover up words and words to hide our thoughts. The title of the play is symbolic of the pattern of life in which the characters are all eventually caught—a great minuet that never ends.

The plot deals with the corruption of an idealistic young man (Valentín) who arrives at court only to be frustrated by the self-interest and plain ignorance of the governing officials when he attempts to implement his ideals. Only the middle-aged minister Gravelot is truly aware of the process that is drawing Valentín into the minuet—just as he himself has learned to move in step with hypocrisy and immorality years before. Also involved in the intrigue is Diana, the pretty young favorite of the king who calls the blundering but amusing monarch "Charlie."

Phyllis Boring has noted the Giraudoux-like humor in *The Grand Minuet* and gives the example of the minister of war who hates war because it destroys gardens, recalling the warning given to the Gardener in *Electre* and the suggestion of Andromaque that flourishing fields attract devastation.[5] Gerald E. Wade, one of the small number of American scholars who have looked closely at the Ruiz Iriarte's theater, questions whether the playwright intended us to view this work as an argument for morality or for indulgent tolerance of vice because human beings are what they are.[6] In general, throughout his career, Ruiz Iriarte has dealt with questions of morality with compassion and insight rather than condemnation. He is, to be sure, a critical observer of hypocrisy and moral ambivalence in a sector of contemporary society, and he has shown particular concern for the sad destruction or compromise of ideals in a society that seems to demand an unconscionable price if ambitions are to be fulfilled.

Juego de niños (A Dangerous Game, 1952)[7] enhanced the author's reputation as an important creator of serious comedy and won for him the National Prize for Drama. It is a work which illustrates particularly well one of Ruiz Iriarte's fundamental dramatic recourses: the *juego* or consciously created deceit which, ironically, approaches or becomes reality. The tampering with reality or truth by the characters may lead to a more authentic awareness of the nature of a relationship or it may produce disaster. The plot of *A Dangerous Game* is simple and direct. The teenage sons (Tony and Manolín) of a well-to-do lawyer (Ricardo) are fully aware of their father's adultery and of the unhappiness their mother (Cándida)[8] tries unsuccessfully to hide. Under the "direction" of a pretty cousin (Maité)l they plan a deceit to cure the father's disinterest. Maité's French tutor (Marcelo) is to pretend to be in love with Cándida to arouse Ricardo's jealousy. But the play-within-the-play begins to take a dangerous turn. Marcelo really loves Cándida and she, in turn, finds herself responding to his gentleness. The playwright shows us the tragic possibilities of the game, but he ends the play on a note of reconciliation.

El pobrecito embustero (The Poor Deceiver), which was staged in 1953, follows closely the aesthetic concepts of *A Dangerous Game*—though it is a somewhat less polished piece of dramatic writing. The play is set in a small provincial city rather than the capital, and the alienation of the main characters is more complex than that of the Del Valle family of the earlier play. The plot is built around three deceits, two of which had been cultivated over a period of years when the play begins; the third "lie" serves as a means of remedying the effects of the first two. Rosalía, the wife of a quiet professor of history (Lorenzo), and her sister Victoria, who lives in America, have built up false images of their respective spouses. Rosalía had spent her honeymoon in Pamplona (just another provincial city), but she had described a romantic trip to Italy in her letters to Victoria. Years pass, and Victoria's son Pedrín arrives in Spain believing that his uncle is a successful army officer rather than an insignificant teacher who is ridiculed by his students. Even the photograph that Rosalía had sent was of another man. Lorenzo confides to Don Julián, a local physician, that he yearns for some indication of authentic love in his life:

LORENZO. I can't go on living this way. This loneliness is overwhelming. . . . There are two words that I would have given a few years of my life just to hear. They're some silly words that were spoken years ago in a theater. It was a play that had a very tender and very pretty love scene. The actress went close to the hero and said to him, very softly, so softly you could scarcely hear her: "My love." Do you understand? It's nothing. Two words. But together they say so much. . . . Are you laughing at me?[9]

Don Julián tells him that his situation could be worse, for their friend Jerónimo is suffering from a fatal illness and has only a month to live. The doctor is taken aback when Lorenzo declares that he would be willing to die if he could have one month of real happiness. Later, when the professor asks the servant Clotilde how she would react in the presence of a man who had only a month to live, the startled girl assumes the worst and immediately informs her mistress of the professor's "illness." As the news spreads through the town, attentions are suddenly heaped upon the "dying" man.

In the second act, Lorenzo realizes that the tributes and concern are not genuine expressions of love or respect. Again he confides in Don Julián:

LORENZO. . . . Do you know something, Don Julián? I've discovered that the sudden love we all feel in the presence of a person who is going to die is not a real love. It's fear. . . . It's fear and remorse for not having loved as much as we should have loved. It's as if in those final hours we wanted to return to them all the affection we have denied them before. . . . And to think that only for the sake of tasting a bit of that love I had the grotesque notion of pretending my own death![10]

He tells his family the truth but decides to enjoy momentarily the celebration that the town has prepared in his honor. When he becomes genuinely ill a short time later, no one believes that he is not pretending. However, the *real* illness is confirmed and Rosalía comes to understand the foolishness of her own misguided deceptions.

Ruiz Iriarte sometimes calls his plays *farsas* rather than *comedias* (which translates into English simply as "play"). In the case of *The Poor Deceiver* he is also referring obliquely to the "farce of life." Although there are scenes of exaggerated humor or satire (such as the appearance of a motion picture actress who wants Lorenzo to die in her arms), the larger farce is filled with tragic implications. At the time of the premiere, one critic called the play a *farsa de costumbres* ("a comedy, or satire, on everyday life") and placed the author within the Spanish tradition of dark humor. He made an apt distinction between this type of theater in Spain and its French counterpart, noting that the latter is impregnated with vaudeville and boulevard comedy whereas in Spain the element of tragicomedy is present.[11]

Over the next few years, Ruiz Iriarte wrote a number of well-crafted and entertaining works that generally found audience approval. But not until 1958 did he offer a new work that represented a change in his dramatic perspectives. *Esta noche es la vispera* (Tonight is the Prelude) is a serious drama of moralistic tone in which the playwright assembles a group of disparate characters whose lives touch because they happen to have taken the same airplane for Paris. Some are running away from responsibility or a situation that has become untenable; others are tempted by promises of greater happiness or success. The flight is grounded in a snow storm, and the passengers have one night in which time is suspended figuratively, if not technically, to reconsider their actions. The events of the decisive night are related in flashback, a technique the playwright uses more imaginatively in several subsequent plays. Although *Tonight is the Prelude* deals convincingly with the questions of conscience and free will, the author's estimate of human capacities for self-redemption may seem overly optimistic in a particularly cynical age.

Some of Ruiz Iriarte's most expert writing has been achieved in the past decade. *El carrusell* (The Carousel, 1964), *La señora recibe una carta* (A Letter Comes, 1967), and *Historia de un adulterio* (Story of a Deceit, 1968) all rank among the best efforts of his career. *The Carousel*—while representing a synthesis of the playwright's major dramatic concerns and techniques—is a direct descendant of *A Dangerous Game.* Daniel Sandoval, the protagonist of the play, is middle-aged and successful; his wife Rita is attractive and totally involved in a whirlwind of social activities, with their concomitant frivolity and intrigues. As their four children (Maribel, Tomy, Ramonín, and Lolín) approach adulthood, they are becoming increasingly alienated from their parents and from each other. Maribel has fallen in love with a young engineer whom she met on the subway and desperately wants to confide in her mother; Tomy is having an affair with a gentle young girl (Mónica) who works in the household; Ramonín, an *aficionado* of avant-garde theater, is having an intense relationship (homosexual by implication) with a young Frenchman named Michel. Lolín, the youngest, has noticed that only during periods of illness or crisis do her parents lavish attention or show concern. Like Maité, in *A Dangerous Game*, she plots a *juego* that will "cure" the apparent disinterest of Daniel and Rita. Ramonín will pretend that he is in trouble with the police; Tomy's "lie" will be that he has fathered an illegitimate child; and Lolín will feign illness. But the "drama" that the teenage girl is directing becomes truth in the case of Tomy and Ramonín. Mónica is actually pregnant, and Ramonín is detained, along with Michel and his friends, by the police.

Lólin becomes frightened by her parents' reaction to the crises and—not aware of the real predicaments of her brothers—tells them that it had all been a game. Daniel and Rita eventually realize that the problems are genuine but cannot face up to the full implications of their sons' actions. When Tomy hesitates in his commitment to marry Mónica, the distraught girl rushes out of the house and is killed by a truck. Whether it is an accident or intentional suicide can never be determined. While Rita eases back into her social activities and plans the wedding of Maribel to her engineer, Daniel has been changed and seeks to understand the tragedy of Mónica's death.

The opening scene of *The Carousel* takes place a year after the tragedy. A jovial police inspector (perhaps inspired by a similar character in Priestley's *An Inspector Calls*) arrives to accept Daniel Sandoval's "confession." The events of the past are presented in flashback, though in normal time sequence. In the third scene, the action returns momentarily to the present to permit Daniel to explain to the Inspector his difficult struggle to achieve success and the meaningless life in which he has been caught:

DANIEL. I have found success, wealth, power. But, of course, so many things have been lost in the struggle! Is that the reason . . . Inspector, that my wife and I are wrapped in a life of frivolity? Can it be that frivolity is the sum of many disillusionments? Is it the loss of hope? Does frivolity replace our lost faith? What can we believe in—those of us who know that almost everything is bought and almost everything is sold, who have bought and sold so many things? If all that is true, then frivolity is a kind of suicide and the world is full of dead men.[12]

In the final scene, the time is again the present. The Inspector tells the remorseful Daniel that it was the *juego* that killed Mónica, the game that does not have an identifiable criminal but which claims its victim nonetheless. In a poetic speech that explains the symbolism of the play's title, the Inspector describes the reason for his appearance in the first place:

INSPECTOR. Life is like an immense, overwhelming carnival. A beautiful, shiny carousel, adorned with colored lights. . . . Magic, fascinating, blinding lights. The carousel is always moving. Day and night. It's like an enchanted world. A paradise of marvels. But suddenly, one day—no one knows why—the carnival is suspended. The great carousel stops. The lights go out. There is endless night . . . and then a man who is afraid calls out . . . I come. . . . Sometimes he doesn't even see me. But I listen to him. Suddenly the carnival comes to life again with all its splendor and noise. The great carousel starts up again . . . and we hear the music. . . .
DANIEL. And then?
INSPECTOR. And then? Nothing. Everything starts all over again.[13]

Rita resumes her life of frivolity, confident that Ramonín will outgrow his inclinations and that Tomy will eventually love a woman of his own social background. There is no assurance that the children will not become participants in the same carnival as their parents. Only Daniel has achieved a degree of self-realization from Mónica's death. Ruiz Iriarte leaves no doubt that he has written a drama of social commentary and that Sandoval is the central character of the work. In a special prologue written for the textbook edition of *The Carousel*, he states:

This play is, in synthesis, . . . a pure and simple result of my private observations of Spanish society of my time. Naturally—let us be humble, honest and truthful in the measuring of our abilities—it is not *all* of

Spanish society that appears reflected in this dramatic situation. . . . It is a sector of that society that is contemplated here, a certain world . . . frivolous and unconcerned, a peculiar manner of understanding life, which, when all is said and done, is perhaps a way of not understanding it. But this is what has produced, among the people of my generation, men like this Daniel Sandoval who go through life bearing the burden of their triumph and of their failure. This character who—although he may not seem so at times—is the real protagonist of the drama hidden in the diverting apparatus of the farce.[14]

In *A Letter Comes*, Ruiz Iriarte dispensed with farce completely to present a thought-provoking confrontation among a group of friends whose dinner party is interrupted by a mysterious anonymous letter. At the beginning of the play, we see five of the six guests at the apartment of the dramatist Alberto Roldán and his wife Adela. They are successful but bored individuals: Laura, a mature actress who has reached the pinnacle of her career; Tomás, a motion picture director with a passion for flashy cars; Alicia, his less-than-brilliant wife; Manuel, a prominent businessman; and his wife Teresa. Later they are joined by Alberto's young secretary, Marina. To break the monotony of their evening, Adela suggests that they play the game of "truth" in which each person must tell what he really thinks of the others. There is even a brief discussion of a drive of a few hundred kilometers to Sevilla for breakfast. Finally, Alberto decides to entertain his guests by reading his new play, but just as he is beginning the doorbell rings. A maid delivers an envelope on which a single phrase is written: "For the wife." The letter itself contains only a question: "Do you know that your husband's lover is in your house tonight?" The audience is kept in suspense as to the actual contents of the note, for when Adela reads it she lets it fall to the floor without disclosing the cause of her consternation. When Alberto picks the letter up to read it, we see only his reaction. But Alicia is bold enough to read it aloud for the benefit of the other guests (and, of course, for the audience).

Three of the women present had either loved Alberto or had been intimate with him. A fourth, Marina, adores him and could well become his mistress in the near future (fulfilling the implication of the note). For each of them the writer has been a different man. Unconsciously they begin to play the game of truth that Adela had suggested earlier, and their deeper interrelationships are brought to light. When the concierge appears and announces that the letter had been intended for another apartment, Adela destroys the missive rather than permit further harm from its explosive question. The party dissolves, but the friends—with the exception of Marina, who has been saved by the series of revelations—return one by one. They recognize that the past binds them together, that the disclosures of their several "truths" have not irrevocably alienated them. The play ends as Alberto sits down once more to begin the reading of his new drama.

A Letter Comes is one of Ruiz Iriarte's most subtle and enjoyable works. However, the title of the play (literally: "The Wife Receives a Letter") is perhaps an unfortunate choice. Although it does describe the event on which the action hinges, it fails to suggest the psychological and intellectual qualities of a drama in which the author demonstrates with fine dramatic skills that the line between reality and illusion is not easily recognized and that truth is multiple, while bringing his characters to a more authentic understanding of their own special interrelationships.

Story of a Deceit is a mature drama that treats the question of conscience and the obstacles a man faces when he determines to discover the unembellished truth of his moral dilemma. Ernesto Luján, a successful banker (not unlike other wealthy, middle-aged characters in Ruiz Iriarte's plays), creates a furor when he calls together his wife (Adelaida), his mistress (Rosalía), and the mistress's husband (Jorge) to announce that he plans to leave the financial world and divide all his holdings among his employees. That these four could be together socially in the first place is the result of their capacities for ignoring or recreating truth. Ernesto suffers a disturbing attack of illness, and an elderly physician is summoned. The action of the play begins just after the doctor has completed his diagnosis, and throughout the drama he serves as a one-man audience for the other characters who recreate the events that led up to Ernesto's declaration. Above all, the banker seeks to find out if Jorge realizes that Rosalía is Ernesto's mistress and that without her intercession, his rapid rise in the bank would have been impossible. But Jorge's compromise has involved a creation of his own "truth" that erases the reality of his wife's adultery. At the end of the play, Adelaida and Ernesto look honestly at the failure of their own relationship as an episode from their youth is replayed before them by a young actor and actress.

Structurally, *Story of a Deceit* is Ruiz Iriarte's most complex work. Present and past are effectively interwoven to form a tight dramatic whole; the characters move back and forth in time simply by taking a few steps across the stage. The play is not devoid of humor (the doctor is presented as a somewhat blundering and unkempt practitioner, for example), but the overall tone is serious. The "farce of life" so basic to the playwright's aesthetic view is still present but it is not accompanied by the pure theatrical farce which frequently covers the serious implications of Ruiz Iriarte's plays.

During the 1960's, the author also continued to write works in a lighter vein. *Un paraguas bajo la lluvia* (An Umbrella Under the Rain, 1965), a genuine farce with occasional touches of pathos, showed the evolution of amorous relationships over a period of several generations. *La muchacha del sombrerito rosa* (The Girl in the Little Pink Hat, 1966) dealt sentimentally with the return of an exiled intellectual to Spain and his reunion with the love of his youth. A sequel to this highly successful comedy, *Primavera en la Plaza de París* (Springtime in the Plaza de París), was staged in 1968. While both plays are written with taste, the political convictions of the principals are presented as modified and softened by the passage of time—which was perhaps a message that that much of the theater public wished to hear.

The theater of Víctor Ruiz Iriarte has been underestimated on occasion.[15] Although he has not ventured into unexplored theatrical terrain, he is one of the best dramatic craftsmen of the contemporary stage. His work clearly bears the stamp of individuality; and like Anouilh in France, with whom he shares a common Pirandellian affinity, he employs a dramatic formula that reveals a recurring personal view of life theatricalized and touched with irony. If he sometimes errs in the direction of sentimentality, it is invariably an honest sentimentality permeated with a fine sense of the poetical. The fact that his great popularity has been associated with his lighter comedies should not be allowed to obscure the value of his more substantial accomplishments.

II *Antonio Buero-Vallejo*

Antonio Buero-Vallejo (b. 1916) is the finest dramatic talent to appear in Spain since the civil war; quite possibly he will prove to be the major Spanish writer of his time. Born in the Castilian city of Guadalajara, he grew up in a home where artistic creativity was respected. In 1934, at the age of eighteen, he went to Madrid to study art, and during the civil war he served in the medical corps of the republic. When the war ended, he was imprisoned for six years—an experience that could only leave a lifelong impression on his thought. After his release in 1945, he abandoned plans for a career as a painter and turned to the theater. When recognition came in 1949 with the production of *Historia de una escalera* (Story of a Stairway), he had already written three full-length works and a one-act play. Both *En la ardiente oscuridad* (In the Burning Darkness) and *Story of a Stairway* were entries in the Lope de Vega competition; the second of the two—the first social drama of consequence in the postwar period—was the winner. *In the Burning Darkness* was staged in 1950; the one-act *Palabras en la arena* (Words in the Sand) was first performed by an amateur group in 1949; but *Aventura en lo gris* (Adventure in Grayness), because of its political concerns, was not produced until 1963.

Story of a Stairway is a realistic drama dealing with the hopes and failures of three generations of inhabitants of a shabby apartment building in Madrid. All of the action takes place on the stairway or landing outside the main doors of four apartments. It is evidence of Buero's native dramatic skills and imaginative powers that a work in which the characters' encounters are limited to meetings on the stairway outside their homes has virtually no awkward moments or transitions. The time of the first act is around 1910, that of the second ten years later, and the third is contemporary with the period of the play's composition. The stairway itself is a unifying element and an indelible visual symbol of the lives of the characters who can only move within boundaries dictated by social conditions or by their own self-delusion. García Pavón has described an even wider symbolic function for Buero's stairway. "[It] is not only a character, as Marquerie sees it; it is something more: the symbol of the immobility of our social organization that prevents a more fluid evolution of our existing hierarchic structure."[16] At the end of the play, Fernando and Carmina (two young lovers who represent the third generation) seek to escape from the endless climbing and descending of the stairs by leaving the building. There is, of course, some element of hope, and the movement away from the stairway suggests that free will can play a role in breaking the cycle of frustrated ambitions. But Buero leaves us with only that possibility; there are no stated or implied assurances that the idealism of the new generation will not be destroyed by the social obstacles that also exist on the outside.[17]

For all its acknowledged merits and its superiority to most of the dramatic works being written in Spain during the late 1940's, *Story of a Stairway* is not the play that provides the most insight into Buero's concepts of drama. A consideration of *In the Burning Darkness* (written before *Stairway*) is fundamental to an understanding of the playwright's ideas and dramatic techniques as they have undergone refinement and grown over more than two decades. The entire action of this vivid drama takes place in a comfortable private institute for blind youths that might well exist in any country. Buero does not specify the locale, but the characters are easily recognizable as products of a bourgeois background. The students have developed a sense of security under the guidance of their jovial "director" (Don Pablo) whose reiterated message is that the blind can accomplish all that is within the province of the sighted and that there is no place for despair in his school. It amounts to a faith that admits no dissent. However, the tranquility of this protected society is disrupted by the appearance of a rebellious young man (Ignacio) who arrives at the beginning of the school year dressed in black, unkempt, and dependent on his cane (a forbidden aid in the institution). With open contempt for what he calls "showers of happiness," he rejects the euphemisms *vidente* ("seer") and *invidente* ("non-seer") that the blind society employs to avoid the word *ciego* ("blind"). It is Ignacio, accepting the terrible reality of his condition and yearning to see, who is the true "vidente" or "seer," for he senses the mysteries beyond the great window that dominates the stage and symbolizes the separateness of the blind world from the glimmers of light.

The threat that Ignacio poses to the stability of the institution becomes so great that Don Pablo suggests to Carlos, the chief spokesman for the students, that Ignacio be persuaded to leave—a suggestion that leads to Carlos's decision to murder the dissenter (who is also his rival in love). The drama ends on a chilling note, with the murderer groping his way to the body of his victim, touching the dead boy's face, and then turning to the window to repeat the exact words spoken by Ignacio earlier in the play when he had challenged Carlos's ideas of conformity:

CARLOS. Out there the stars are shining in all their splendor, and men with sight know their marvelous presence. Those far-off worlds, beyond the window. (*His hands tremble and beat against the mysterious prison of glass like the wings of a wounded bird.*) Within reach of our sight! . . . if we could see. . .[18]

In the Burning Darkness is a play with some defects; for example, in the dialogue of the female characters (with the exception of the sighted Doña Pepita) whose reactions to Ignacio remain exclusively on the emotional level. But in its totality it is a remarkable first play by any criterion—all the more so when one considers the circumstances of the inexperienced author's life that immediately preceded its composition. In the work there are dramatic devices that have remained constant in Buero's theater while being continually refined as he breaks away from the traditional three-act structure utilized for all but one of his early efforts.[19] The visual symbols—such as the great window, and the chess board set up in the final act with the chessmen all in place until they are knocked over by an unintentional movement of Carlos's arm—are part of the playwright's concept of a theater that integrates the visual and the verbal with sounds and music to achieve a total dramatic appeal to the mind and to the senses. As in virtually all his subsequent works, music and specific sounds are essential parts of the dramatic fabric. In *Burning Darkness*, the *Moonlight* Sonata of Beethoven and a section of Grieg's incidental music for *Peer Gynt* serve for more than mere mood or background effect, and the sound of a kiss heard by the blind director and Carlos is used for a striking dramatic purpose. Most important of all, perhaps, is the tentative use of what Buero calls *interiorización*. The stage is temporarily darkened to place the audience in direct participation at the moment Ignacio is attempting to explain the torment resulting from a total absence of light. Admittedly, it is an artificial device in this early work;

but later it is employed consummately in *El concierto de San Ovidio* (The Concert at Saint Ovide) in the murder scene, in *El sueño de la razón* (The Sleep of Reason) in terms of sound, and, most extensively, in *La llegada de los dioses* (the Arrival of the Gods), where the distorted and grotesque inner vision of the young blind painter, Julio, is conveyed by a refinement of the same technique.

Adventure in Grayness might possibly have served to give Buero an international reputation had it been translated and performed at the time his work was first recognized in Spain. This play was published in its original version in 1954 in the theater review *Teatro,* but censorship and the caution of commercial producers prevented its performance for more than a decade. When it was finally staged in 1963—a time of censorship relaxation—a revised and somewhat more forceful version was used. The work deals with the confrontation of a liberal intellectual (Silvano) and a deposed dictator (Goldmann) at the moment their country (called Surelia) is about to fall to an invading army. With several other refugees from the war, they spend a night of hunger and violence in an abandoned inn. The ex-dictator murders one of the refugees—a young woman with a child that has been fathered by an enemy soldier. Silvano and Goldmann's mistress (Ana) remain with the infant, knowing that they face death from the invaders. But before they walk out to be shot, they have the assurance that the child will survive.

Despite the acclaim for *Story of a Stairway* and the less enthusiastic but respectful reception of *In the Burning Darkness,* in the early years of his career Buero did not enjoy either financial success or appropriate recognition of his importance to a new and evolving Spanish theater. On the contrary, several of his plays had very limited runs, and from time to time there were opinionated and unfair personal attacks against him. Although no play that he wrote in this period was without demonstrable intellectual and theatrical interest, it was not until he began his cycle of historical dramas in 1958 that Buero freed himself sufficiently from conventional theatrical modes to reveal the true dimensions of his dramatic vision.

The production of *In the Burning Darkness* was followed in 1952 by *La tejedora de sueños* (The Dream Weaver),[20] a play based on the legend of Penelope's long and faithful wait for

Ulysses as he was experiencing the adventures of *The Odyssey*. Antiwar in sentiment, the work provides an effective contrast between the intellectual spirit of a man of peace and the arrogant soldier. The drama ends with Penelope pretending to be the loyal wife of Ulysses but bearing within her the sorrow for the death of Amphion, the younger man who had reawakened her capacity for love. *La señal que se espera* (The Sign We Wait For), also produced in 1952, is an engrossing but dramatically uneven piece which treats the problem of a composer (Luis) who has lost his power of creativity after suffering a mental breakdown. He believes that by some miracle the melody that he has forgotten will be played by the wind on an aeolian harp. His former love, Susanna, plays the melody and provides the means for Luis's regeneration. Eventually the composer realizes that human assistance had given back to him his artistic power. In a subplot, two elderly servants in the household of Susanna and her husband Enrique await a letter from their estranged nephew in America and believe that the sound of the harp will be a sign that their hopes will be realized. But instead of the expected communication from the young man, they receive news of his death in an accident.

Joelyn Ruple ranks *The Sign We Wait For* low among the playwright's accomplishments and believes the play represents a concession to a Catholic society. She suggests that Buero has tried to please the public by talking about miracles in which he does not really believe in a manner that will not offend those who do and that he felt no personal sense of identification with the talented middle-class characters he has portrayed.[21] However, if the dramatist was trying to please the public, he did not succeed. On the opening night, the third act was interrupted by the *pateo* ("stamping") with which Spanish audiences express their displeasure. The final act was immediately revised—though without producing a wholly satisfactory dramatic experience.[22] In a commentary for the published version of the work, the playwright wrote in defense of an ending that did not result in disaster for his protagonist: "Tragedy does not necessarily lead to a final catastrophe, but is rather a special way of looking at a result, be it happy or bitter. Someday, with better implements than this time, I shall attempt a work which can be subtitled, unequivocally, *'tragedia feliz'* ["a positive, or hopeful, tragedy"]"[23]

Casi un cuento de hadas (Almost a Fairy Tale, 1953) is a free dramatic treatment of Charles Perrault's seventeenth-century tale of Riquet, the ugly prince who loves a beautiful but supposedly insensitive princess. Though not a major work (it had only nineteen performances), *Almost a Fairy Tale* is by no means inferior in design or composition to other plays of the early years of Buero's career. In their respective books on the playwright, both Joelyn Ruple and Martha Halsey have provided thoughtful analyses which serve to remedy the neglect the play has suffered and to reveal it as a worthy demonstration of Buero's thought and techniques. The title is perhaps deceptive, but the word "almost" is the key to the dramatist's approach to the "beauty and the beast" theme. Basing his action on a familiar mythic situation, he has produced a serious consideration of the complexities of human love, illusion, the search for the ideal, and the relationship between outward physical qualities and inner personality. Two actors, who are seen onstage simultaneously on occasion, are used effectively to portray the prince so that he appears both in his actual ugliness and as transformed by illusion and love. The ultimate resolution is not a happy "fairy tale" ending; rather Leticia, the princess, abandons her illusion to accept the reality of the Riquet that the world sees, even though such an acceptance is accompanied by both suffering and the memory of an unobtainable ideal.

Madrugada (Dawn, 1953) proved to be one of the most popular of Buero's early works and was made into a reasonably effective motion picture version. Critics are not completely in agreement as to the artistic value of this drama, with attitudes ranging from extreme admiration (Giuliano) to a very reserved appreciation (Torrente Ballester and Ruple). Undeniably, it is a skillfully wrought dramatic piece; at the same time it lacks the theatrical impact and breadth of a number of subsequent plays by the author. It is a tight, suspenseful drama dealing with the efforts of Amalia, wife and former mistress of a prominent artist who has just died, to discover the reasons behind her husband's apparent coldness to her after their marriage and for his disinheriting certain close relatives. *Dawn* provides some of the clearest examples of the influence of Ibsen in Buero's theater; and, as Martha Halsey has shown,[24] parallels between *Dawn* and Ibsen's *Ghosts* are particularly notable. Both plays have a protagonist who undertakes a tragic search for truth about herself and about the past; and the symbolic stage effect of light flooding the room at the end of *Dawn* corresponds to Ibsen's use of sunlight on the mountains in *Ghosts*. Without question, the most admirable quality of the play is its remarkably controlled form. The unities are strictly observed while a conspicuous clock records literally the playing time of the two acts as Amalia, working against time, seeks her answers. Halsey expresses admiration for Buero's achievement and finds in the work "perfect fusion of subject and form, the same integrated structure of Sophoclean tragedy."[25]

Irene o el tesoro (Irene or the Treasure, 1954) is the dramatist's most complex and most ambitious effort of the mid-1950's. Because of the introduction of a supernatural element in the person of a *duende* (which means "spirit," "elf," "fairy," etc., but lacks a really precise English equivalent) and a double plane of reality presented onstage, a convincing performance of the play (or a satisfactory translation into English) is not easy to achieve in spite of its strong dramatic appeal. The published edition is prefaced with a line from a poem by Unamuno: "El secreto del alma redimida: vivir los sueños al soñar la vida." ("The secret of the redeemed soul: to live dreams while dreaming life".) It provides a key to the understanding of Irene, the widowed and childless woman who is visited by a strange, childlike spirit in the midst of her emotional and physical deprivation. The play ends with a splendidly theatrical scene depicting the transcendental reality of Irene, as she moves singing along a mysterious road of light, and the reality of the world she is leaving, where her body has been discovered in the street. No résumé can suggest the power of this unusual combination of harsh reality and poetic vision. The work is enigmatic, and acceptance of the enigma is of the essence in an appreciation of its dramatic values.

Hoy es fiesta (Today's a Holiday, 1956) won both the María Rolland Drama Prize and the National Drama Award. Called a "tragicomedy in three acts," the play deals with the importance of hope to the survival of a group of characters who live in an environment not unlike that of the inhabitants of the *casa de vecindad* in *Story of a Stairway*. But Buero's return to the impoverished milieu of the earlier play does not result in an imitative drama. The playwright himself maintains that *Today's a Holiday* is as closely related to *In the Burning Darkness* in spirit and technique as it is to *Story of a Stairway* in setting. He has also pointed out that Silverio, a principal figure in the play, is very close to the blind Ignacio in his inner tension and that both protagonists determine the ultimate meaning of the works in which they appear.[26]

Although the action of the play is confined to the rooftop of a tenement, the interrelationships of the numerous characters are complex. Within the collective tragedy of the tenement dwellers and their hope of escaping their physical sordidness by winning a lottery prize, it is the individual struggle of Silverio to find self-understanding and to reach his wife Pilar through the barrier of her literal and symbolic deafness that provides a focal point for the action. Some critics have not looked far beyond the outward realism of this work, but Martha Halsey has noted the metaphysical intent that underlies the action (as well as the involved symbolism), and correctly concludes that the hunger of the characters is spiritual as well as material, that their inner search is revealed in their eagerness to ascend to the tenement roof (which is normally off-limits) in order to breathe "a purer, loftier air."[27] Although there is no way to climb higher than the roof, the characters are at least touched by light—both literally and symbolically.

Las cartas boca abajo (The Cards Face Down), produced the following year, provided further evidence of Buero's growing command of his materials. The play is set in the shabby apartment of a middle-aged professor (Juan) who is experiencing the ordeal of the series of eliminating examinations for a university post in Spain. To regain his own self-esteem and redeem a life of mediocrity, he must win over the other candidates. His wife (Adela) despises the life that her marriage has brought and entertains illusions of a more glamorous existence. The man who had rejected her (Carlos Ferrer) before her marriage to Juan is now a leading intellectual; and, ironically, Juan's stubborn refusal to become acquainted with Ferrer's writings contributes to his failure in the competition. Also a part of the household is an older sister (Anita) who had been in love with Ferrer only to see him become infatuated with Adela. Anita now lives in self-imposed silence. She is ever present as the conscience of Adela and openly expresses her affection for Juan and for her nephew Juanito by small attentions and gestures. Mauro, the irresponsible brother of the two women, frequents the apartment and meddles in the family crisis by pretending to know Ferrer and to have sufficient influence to convince him to intercede in the competition on Juan's behalf. After being eliminated, Juan momentarily allows his family to believe that he has won. Juanito proves that Mauro could not have spoken to Ferrer and achieves a reconciliation with his father. Adela is left alone with the mute but accusing Anita. *The Cards Face Down* is a drama of silent agonies, buried anger, and debilitating resentments which eventually surface in highly charged confrontations as the cards are turned face up. Although basically realistic, the plays contains a rather eerie poetic effect in the chirping of the birds that Adela hears—at first symbolizing the freedom and joy that she longs for and later her terror.

After the production of *The Cards Face Down*, Buero freed himself from the restrictions of the single-set play and turned to a new source of inspiration to produce a series of impressive dramas based loosely on historical characters or events. The first, *Un soñador para un pueblo* (A Dreamer for a People, 1958), dealt with the reforming efforts of the Marqués de Esquilache, an eighteenth-century political figure not widely known outside Spain. Born in Italy, Esquilache (Squillaci in Italian) was brought to Spain by Carlos III to replace the minister Ensenada. In Buero's play he is depicted as a visionary who is opposed by the conservative forces. An uprising against the minister's reforms is instigated by the rival Ensenada. Esquilache must ultimately accept exile but his "vision" of an improved society for the people of Spain transcends his own personal sacrifice. As in earlier, less elaborate works of Buero, sounds and visual symbols are essential elements of the dramatic structure. And the playwright's concept of inner vision and its power to move men from darkness to light (or at least an initimation of it) is movingly conveyed in the dialogue and in the complementary visual effects.

Before his imprisonment at the end of the Spanish civil war, Buero had been an art student, so it is hardly surprising that three of his major plays have dealt with painters. His second historical work, *Las Meninas* (1960), presents the mature Diego

Velázquez caught in a web of political and sexual intrigue at the time he is making the preliminary sketches for the painting which will become his greatest achievement. Faced with the prudery of his wife, the sexual envy of his apprentice (Juan de Pareja), and the professional envy of other painters, Velázquez finds himself an alienated genius incapable of communicating his vision of the mysteries of light to anyone except the aged and half-blind revolutionary Pedro, who had served many years before as a model for the painting called "Aesop." At one point he shows his sketches for the painting "Las Meninas" to the old man and describes the figures he intends to paint as "beings saved by light"—that is, given immortality through colors on canvas which can only exist through light—and he adds: "I have come to suspect that the very form of God—if he has any form—must be light."[28] Paradoxically, it is the physically sightless Pedro who becomes the seer (or who is, at least, capable of a glimmer of understanding).

Velázquez survives the accusations of the Inquisition and defends himself before his king, Felipe IV. But Pedro, the single being who shares the power of vision, throws himself to his death to avoid capture, torture, and incrimination of the painter as his protector. The play ends with a tableau which recreates precisely the scene depicted in the painting known as "Las Meninas." Martin, another former model of Velázquez, serves as a Brechtian commentator to the audience and as an interpreter of the action. At this moment he functions as stage director as each character speaks his own thoughts. The final word of the dialogue is the name of the martyred Pedro, spoken twice by the painter as he accepts a condition of spiritual exile and aloneness.

Buero's second play in which blindness is a paramount consideration is *The Concert at Saint Ovide* (1962). Although this too is one of the cycle of historical plays, the characters, with one exception, are the creations of the playwright's imagination suggested by an eighteenth-century etching advertising an actual performance of a group of blind musicians at the Fair of Saint Ovide in Paris in 1771. Buero calls the work "a parable in three acts," and it does indeed reflect the social injustices of our own time which create a desperate sense of alienation among our artistic nonconformists. Six blind beggars who reside at a refuge for the blind originally established in the thirteenth century are contracted to perform for the impresario Valindin at his restaurant during the Saint Ovide Fair. One of the six, David, is a visionary who rejects the role assigned to the blind and speaks of the rumors he has heard of a sightless noblewoman who has learned to read; and he also believes that it is possible for the blind to become skilled musicians, capable of playing harmony rather than scraping out a single melodic line. Valindin, the epitome of the capitalist entrepreneur, does not consider himself an exploiter of men and praises his own philanthropy. He neglects to explain to the blind men that he really wants them to appear ridiculous, to wear fools' costumes, and to sing erotic ditties. David protests when he discovers the truth, but he is helpless to prevent the "concert." When he can no longer tolerate Valindin's inhumanity, he kills the impresario in total darkness, in a scene that represents Buero's refinement of the technique of *interiorización* which compels the audience to share the terror of the deed rather than react to it across an imaginary barrier. Tragically, David is betrayed to the police by Donato, the blind boy he loves like a son, and he is hanged.

A striking aspect of the structure of *Concert at Saint Ovide* is the introduction of a single historical character, Valentin Haüy, the actual teacher of Louis Braille, who was to perfect a system which permits the blind to read. Haüy participates briefly in the action at the end of the second act, witnessing the "concert" and becoming enraged at the mockery the blind musicians are forced to endure. He appears again only at the end of the play to speak directly to the audience in an epilogue that recalls the events of the thirty years that have elapsed since David's arrest: the French Revolution, the destruction of those who made the revolution, and his own dedication to the education of the blind. At no time has he had knowledge more than hearsay of the fate of the six musicians; but as he is speaking, we see onstage David's betrayer Donato, now an old man who wanders the streets, always playing the single composition he had learned from David. Like Carlos in *Burning Darkness*, Donato has inherited a part of another's vision, and his life has been filled with remorse for his impetuous act. Haüy ponders the fate of the blind man who was hanged (he doesn't even know his name), and he suggests that only within creativity can we hope to find some understanding of man's suffering:

HAÜY. It's true that I'm opening up new lives for the blind children in my school. But if it's true that they hanged one of those blind musicians, who will answer for that death? I'm an old man now. Sometimes, when I'm alone as I am now, I like to wonder if perhaps . . . if perhaps music is not the only answer to some questions.[29]

In his study of Buero's theater, Robert Nicholas states that Valentin Haüy is moved to devote his life to helping the blind through the catharsis resulting from witnessing the "performance" at the Saint Ovide Fair.[30] He does not note, however, that the catharsis experienced by Haüy during the concert-within-the-play is achieved without knowledge of the identities and individual tragedies of the blind men. What he witnesses is a collective social tragedy. On the other hand, the audience for Buero's complete play is involved in the individual sufferings of the doomed lovers, David and Adriana, and of their betrayer Donato. The reappearance of Haüy in the epilogue of the play has been criticized, but it is precisely through this reappearance that Buero is able to link the personal tragedies with the wider social tragedy.

When *Concert at Saint Ovide* was first performed, Spain's most demanding theater critics joined in praise for the play. Juan Emilio Aragonés called it "the first great tragedy of Spanish theater of all time."[31] José Monleón detected some influence from Brecht's works—particularly from *Arturo Ui,* in which the German playwright had attacked the evils of Nazism by means of a story of Chicago gangsters—as well as elements of the *esperpento* of Valle-Inclán.[32] Curiously, he did not comment at the time on the most unmistakably Buerian scene of the play: the murder of Valindin in total darkness. Structurally, *Concert at Saint Ovide* is a less than perfect play. The first act is overly long, with certain speeches becoming excessively wordy; and the appearances and reappearances of characters whose function is to illustrate the attitudes or condition of different elements of society do not always result in smooth transitions. Similarly, the third act contains some overextended passages of dialogue. But in the extraordinarily powerful second act Buero demonstrates his dramatic inventiveness to the fullest. After a brief but important introductory scene between Valindin's mistress Adriana and the six blind musicians, the performers are brought to the café to be dressed in striking but outlandish costumes. Violence erupts when David refuses to put on the fool's hat and comic glasses. When the terrified Donato pleads with him to obey Valindin, he accedes for the boy's sake. The "audience," which includes Valentin Haüy, appears and the "concert" begins. Through three verses of a stupid song about a shepherdess and her erotic desires, the raucousness of the onlookers increases—interrupted after the second section of the song by an outburst from Haüy who refuses to participate further in what he considers to be an outrageous abuse of the afflicted musicians. At the end of the act, the audience is bleating like sheep in mockery of the song, and we realize that they have been transformed into dehumanized beasts. It is the realization of this crucial scene that determines above all the effectiveness of any performance of this work.

Buero has acknowledged the influence of Ibsen on his concepts of theater, and his early dramas reveal his affinity with the Norwegian dramatist in their symbolic structures. Even though *A Dreamer for a People*, *Las Meninas*, and *The Concert at Saint Ovide* represent an expansion of the playwright's techniques (specifically, in the direction of total theater), the introduction of elements of distancing, and an overall widening of his dramatic vision, the double plane of reality and symbolism is an essential quality of these historical tragedies and can be seen as a tie with the more conventionally structured dramas that preceded them.

Buero's next work, *La doble historia del Doctor Valmy* (The Double Case History of Doctor Valmy) was completed in 1964 but encountered censorship problems when it was presented for consideration. It still remains unperformed and unpublished in Spain. However, the play has been performed in Farris Anderson's English version in England and published in a textbook edition in Spanish in the United States. It represents a return to a contemporary setting, and the action is placed in the fictitious country of Surelia (which the author had invented for *Adventure in Grayness* years before). The work deals forcefully with injustice and the deterioration of human values in a modern police state, presenting the effect on both the adherents of the state and their victims. Sexual pathology, new to Buero's theater, is a critical element in the dramatic development. Giuliano considers *Doctor Valmy* to be the best work Buero had written at that time.[33] Though it is clearly a drama of quality, this is a personal judgment that can be debated—given the extraordinary intellectual and dramatic vision that are evidenced in the three historical dramas that preceded it.

With *El tragaluz* (Basement Skylight, 1967) Buero enjoyed both public and critical acceptance of one of his strongest efforts. No doubt the unusual public appeal could be attributed in part to this drama's uncompromising treatment of events that had taken place during the civil war and their effect upon the lives of the principal characters. The play opens in the distant future, at a time when technology has provided a method for replaying actions of the past to reevaluate their significance; but the central action takes place in the present and deals with a conflict within a contemporary Spanish family stemming from a traumatic separation suffered during the chaotic period of the war. The use of sound and lighting effects is the most elaborate that the playwright had yet attempted and points toward still greater concern for the integration of the visual and sound elements to complement dialogue and action.

Mito (Myth), published in 1968, is not a play but rather a libretto for an opera that has not yet been composed.[34] The nature of the dramatic development requires that both traditional musical form and electronic music be employed in the score (there is an "opera-within-the-opera" in traditional mold as well as scenes which represent the presence of extraterrestrial beings). Written in verse, it is a complex treatment of the Quixote-Sancho Panza theme, with the modern Quixote being a decrepit actor who sees visions of superior beings from Mars. Just as the famous knight of Cervantes is deceived by an ordinary man dressed in resplendent armor, the actor Eloy is mocked by other actors performing their own depraved version of his illusion. A strong political element is also present in the work, and Eloy ultimately sacrifices his life to save a fugitive from the state police. *Myth* could probably be successfully performed as a verse drama, with the use of music restricted mainly to the opera-within-the-opera and to the Martian scenes; but, hopefully, it will eventually be completed according to the playwright's original intent. There are, to be sure, unmistakable operatic potentialities in other of Buero's works that were not envisioned as musical dramas when they were written. It is not inconceivable that *The Concert at Saint Ovide* and *The Sleep of Reason* (or, for that matter, some of the earlier plays) will attract the interest of operatic composers.

With *El sueño de la razón* (The Sleep of Reason, 1970), Buero returned to visionary historical theater and produced one of the most impressive achievements of his career. It is also the work which has brought him the most international attention to date. (In the fall of 1973, productions of this play were scheduled or being considered in London, Moscow, Warsaw, Prague, and several other European cities.) The protagonist of *The Sleep of Reason* is Francisco de Goya, one of Spain's greatest and most intriguing creative figures of the past. The play deals with his years of physical decline, when his work had taken on the dark and phantasmagoric qualities that some interpreted as the product of senility or even madness. At the beginning of the play, the painter is already seventy-six years old and has endured the agonies of deafness for more than three decades. This provides Buero with the opportunity to employ sound and the absence of sound in the same way that he had used light and darkness in several earlier works. Here we find a startling and innovative dramatic recourse: none of the words spoken in the presence of the deaf painter are audible to the audience—although the sense of each scene is clear from Goya's responses and the sign language or pantomime of the other characters. At the same time, Goya does hear in his mind the wailing of a cat or the howling of a dog (sounds of terror) and his own heart beats, which are heard at varying levels of amplification by the audience in actual performance. Another technique employed with unusual effect is the projection of the drawings and paintings of Goya to complement his thoughts and inner struggle.[35] At the time of the play's events, Ferdinand VII has regained power in Spain and seeks a confession of error from the artist who had once been the royal court painter. In the scenes in which the king appears, he is seen embroidering—an unexpected and somewhat bizarre pastime for a monarch.

Goya is also faced with the frustrations of his young mistress who is the loyal companion of a man whose sexual vigor has declined. Like David, Ignacio, and Velázquez, Goya is portrayed as a visionary. His powers as a seer—interpreted as hallucinations by some—enable him to conceive of men flying through the air at a time when such an action was considered by "non-seers" to be pure fantasy. A principal concern in *The Sleep of Reason* is the effect of fear and repression on the creative mind. In one lengthy monologue (many of the scenes in which Goya appears amount to monologues because of the unheard replies), the painter describes the horrors he has witnessed and the influence of fear and terror upon his art—as illustrated by the dark paintings on the walls of his studio:

GOYA. . . . What do we live for? To paint like this? Fear is oozing from these walls. Fear, yes! And an art that is born from fear cannot be good. . .I delighted in painting beautiful forms, and these are filled with maggots. I drank in all the world's colors, and on these walls shadows are swallowing up those colors. I loved reason, and I paint witches. They are rotting paintings. Yes. In "Asmodea" there is a hope, but so fragile. It is a dream.[36]

The Sleep of Reason is Buero's most difficult work in terms of staging and the one that places the most demands on the audience, which is led by the multimedia aspects of a performance into the very mind of the agonizing Goya. With this play Buero confirmed beyond question his preeminence among Spanish playwrights and sustained his right to be included among the major international dramatic writers of his time.

Buero-Vallejo's next play, *La llegada de los dioses* (The Arrival of the Gods, 1971), is called "a fable in two parts." It is contemporary in setting and treats the alienation of the generations, of son and father, so pronounced in our own time. Julio, a young artist with a modest talent far removed from the perfected skills of a Velázquez, has suddenly gone blind after the failure of his exhibit (which coincided with the success of a showing of works by his father, a conventional and amateurish creator of popular scenes of pagan deities). The young man has also discovered that his father had been a member of the secret police during an unspecified war and had authorized the torture of prisoners. The surviving son of one of the victims, blinded by his captors, has been the source of this information. Julio is intensely aware not only of his father's past guilt but also of the ever-present danger of atomic or ecological disaster. And though he rebels against the complacency of bourgeois society, he cannot totally escape from the influences of the world into which he was born.

The play is complex both in technical devices and in thought. The technique of *interiorización*, requiring intense and even painful audience identification with the blind painter, is employed extensively. Two views of reality are presented: the actual words and actions of the characters, performed in normal fashion when Julio is offstage, and the distorted vision of their appearances and behavior when the young man himself is a part of the stage action. The latter is achieved through the use of masks and lighting effects. Julio has sought true vision in blindness but what he imagines is grotesque and terrifying. In the second half of the play, he begins to experience brief glimmers of light, and for a short time his sight is completely restored—though he continues to feign blindness in the expectation of discovering his lover (Verónica) in an amorous act with his father. Finally, total blindness returns and Julio accepts Verónica as his guide. The young painter lacks the absolute faith in his vision that led Ignacio to destruction in *Burning Darkness*. Since his talent is unproved, he cannot really aspire to be a modern artistic giant (like Velázquez in a different age). His vision is affected by his own fear of twentieth-century man's self-created dangers. But at the end of the play he does break with a society he considers false and sets forth on an uncertain road as Verónica delivers an Unamunian response to his ultimate fear:

JULIO. And if destruction comes first . . .
VERONICA. We shall die on our way![37]

The public reception of *The Arrival of the Gods* was unusually warm for a play of such demanding and somber nature.[38] However, the critical reviews showed mixed feelings about the quality of the work. In an interview with the playwright,[39] Angel Fernández Santos (an admirer of Buero's theater) stated frankly that he considered this play to be a considerable step backward from *The Sleep of Reason* and *Basement Skylight*. He even suggested that *Arrival of the Gods* might have been written earlier in the playwright's career. Buero assured him that his guess was wrong and gave his own differing opinion of the worth of his drama:

> Considering the degree of dissatisfaction that all my efforts produce in me, I feel that this work is not inferior to those that immediately preceded it and that it can be counted among my most important [works] . . . . In my personal trajectory it attempts to continue and extend the dramatic experiences and concerns that inspired the earlier works. You will have seen that, as in *The Sleep of Reason*, I attempt again an interiorization of the audience into the drama through a similar technique: blinding it but making it see the imagined visions of the protagonist—just as in *Sleep* I made the audience deaf but made it hear the fantasies of the protagonist. I believe, then, that this work represents a continuation in a certain personal line of experimentation. Whether it is effective or not is open to debate.[40]

Buero's total theater is rich in themes and associations that invite extensive and detailed investigations. The development of the alienated visionary from Ignacio to David and Julio is obviously fundamental to an understanding of his dramatic aims.[41] Indeed, the expression "visionary drama" might well be used to identify the essence of this playwright's contribution to world theater. There are other intriguing relationships among the female characters in Buero's plays and their special functions as guides to, or inhibitors of, the fulfillment of the men who seek their understanding. In the actual realization of his works, the uses of music (never as mere background) and specific sounds, as well as the ever-present visual symbols, could provide a small catalog of effects which have been employed with increasing mastery by the playwright.[42]

Most important of all in a consideration of Buero's work is his own tragic view of life and his personal concept of tragic theater which permits the element of hope to prevail even in the face of death or failure.[43] His view is, of course, essentially pessimistic, and in most of his plays the protagonist is either defeated or subjected to an irrevocable loss. Although there are examples of inner victory, hope usually lies beyond, in the hands of the inheritors of the sometimes irrational dreams of the defeated or in the durability of the artistic or creative effort. As an unswerving creator of tragic theater, Buero occupies a position that many would consider unique in Spanish letters. When his most recent play, *La fundación* (The Foundation), finally had its premiere in Madrid in January, 1974—after frustrating postponements due to censorial objections—the eminent critic Francisco García Pavón wrote; "[He] is the only pure tragedian in the history of the Spanish theater. Here we almost never had tragic writers nor did tragedy permeate the Spanish sensibility. And with Buero the miracle has been achieved. We have a tragedian and tragedy—this is very important—accepted and vigorously applauded by the public. Perhaps the greatest tragedy of Spain—the last civil war—had to occur before tragedy could take root in our theater through the work of an author of that generation."[44]

III Alfonso Sastre

Alfonso Sastre Salvador was born in Madrid in 1926. Although he has achieved production for fewer of his plays than Buero-Vallejo, his agitation for theater of social consequence, his frequent critical essays on drama and its purposes, and his bold involvement in movements to abolish or modify the institution of censorship in Spain have made him a major force in the modern Spanish theater. Sastre has extended the possibilities for other committed playwrights of his generation while enduring the frustrations of writing plays that were frequently denied performance by the censors.

As a student at the University of Madrid in the late 1940's he began a vigorous criticism of the theatrical establishment and was instrumental in the founding of *Arte Nuevo* (New Art), a group dedicated to the renewal of the stale Spanish theater of those days through the introduction of new forms and ideas. Among the founders of the group was also Alfonso Paso, an aspiring playwright of Sastre's age who would follow a professional road quite divergent from his friend's. Perhaps the most significant accomplishment of *Arte Nuevo* was the publication of a journal called *La hora* (The Hour) in which the ideas and criticisms of the group appeared. *Arte Nuevo* lasted only two years and was succeeded by the *Teatro de agitación social* ("Theater of Social Agitation"), headed by Sastre and José María de Quinto and aiming to present in Spain important foreign dramatists such as

Brecht, Sartre, and O'Neill. While neither *Arte Nuevo* nor the
T.A.S. (which never really became functional) fulfilled its aims or
had any immediate effect on the course of Spanish theater, the
very fact of their existence gave testimony to the important
concern among young intellectuals of creative bent for a renewal
of serious dramatic writing in Spain.

Significant notice was first given to Sastre's talents as a
playwright when a university drama group called T. P. U. (Teatro
Popular Universitario) staged his *Escuadra hacia la muerte* in the
national María Guerrero Theater in 1953. The event was perhaps
even more important than the play itself, for it represented the
first inroad of the new spirit of theater committed to social
awareness. The ovations of an audience that was already prepared
to approve the play were loud, and permission was granted by
the authorities to continue the production. But after the third
performance, the run was suspended. Because of its setting in a
future world war, *Condemned Squad* has lost none of its
immediacy and remains one of Sastre's most interesting dramatic
efforts—if not one of his most consummate in terms of theatrical
values. The play deals with a squad of five soldiers (four of them
bearing a burden of guilt) and their corporal, who find themselves
in a no-man's-land and unable to identify the enemy. In the first
half of the drama, a sense of despair and frustration is created in
the five scenes leading to the crucial sixth scene in which the
brutal corporal is murdered by four of the soldiers on Christmas
Eve. The second part of the play traces the effect of the violent
act upon the guilty men as well as upon the innocent soldier
Luis, who is left at the end with some hope of physical and
spiritual survival. Although antimilitaristic in tone, *Condemned
Squad* is less a statement against the misuse of human beings in
wars that they are unable to comprehend than a study of guilt
and responsibility. Today it is hard to look upon this play as a
subversive work in any sense. And it offers more intellectual
interest than dramatic impact. The murder scene is indeed
overpowering, but it occurs in the middle of the play. In the final
scenes it becomes difficult for actors to sustain interest in the
plight of the soldiers as their group gradually breaks up, leaving
on stage only the young Luis (who did not participate in the
violence) and one of the assassins.

In spite of the attention that came with *Condemned Squad*

Sastre's subsequent works have not found a large audience, and a number of his best plays have been denied performance by the censors or have been shunned by producers. It is not surprising that those works that have been performed have not dealt directly with political themes. However, it should be noted that the playwright himself does not advocate a purely ideological theater. Even in those dramas which do incorporate in some degree the theme of revolution—such as *Guillermo Tell tiene los ojos tristes* (Sad are the Eyes of William Tell), *Tierra roja* (Red Earth), *En la red* (In the Net), and *El pan de todos* (Community Bread)—revolt is not seen as an absolute solution to society's ills. As Farris Anderson has noted in his detailed study of Sastre and his thought,[45] the playwright is aware that revolutionary movements turn reactionary and must be constantly challenged. Thus social freedom is a living and evolving process that can only exist as a struggle between order and anarchy.

Outstanding among the early plays of Sastre which have been published but not staged in Spain is *Sad are the Eyes of William Tell*, in which the dramatist treats the legend of the fourteenth-century Swiss patriot in a highly original manner. Sastre's version alters the familiar story by having Tell actually kill his son when he shoots the apple from his head. There are intentional anachronisms; soldiers appear in modern uniforms and carry modern weapons to emphasize the timelessness of the dramatic conflict between the oppressed and heedless absolutism. The work is divided into seven compact scenes and employs songs to comment directly to the audience. Although Sastre became seriously interested in Brechtian techniques of alienation some years after the writing of *William Tell*, the play does suggest a familiarity with the German playwright's theater and theories of drama.

Sastre's first production in the commercial theater was *La mordaza* (The Gag, 1954), which enjoyed a respectable run of eighty performances. It is also a drama dealing with guilt and moral responsibility. The protagonist of the play, the brutal Isaías Krappo, lives comfortably with his wife, three sons and a daughter-in-law (Luisa). In the opening *cuadro* ("scene"), he is confronted by a man whose wife and daughter had been killed by Krappo during the war. Krappo shoots his accuser, but the crime is witnessed by Luisa—who is also threatened with death if she reveals what she has seen. She shares her knowledge with the sons, but they find themselves gagged by fear or by their own feelings toward their father. Finally, Luisa denounces the criminal herself, and he is killed attempting to escape from prison. Such a dramatic situation might well have appealed to a more conservative writer such as Calvo-Sotelo, but it would have been treated in a more conventional manner. In a series of six terse scenes and an epilogue, Sastre's writing is straightforward and penetrating, and the dramatic interest is unflagging throughout the work.

La sangre de Dios (The Blood of God), a strange, melodramatic, and uneven drama of obsession and violence which provides two outcomes for the same dramatic situation, was performed in Valencia in 1955; however, the production was never seen in Madrid. Two years later, *Community Bread* was presented in Barcelona in a production that was not sanctioned by the playwright. Sastre's next commercial showing in Madrid came in the fall of 1957 with *El cuervo* (The Raven). The title is derived from Edgar Allan Poe's well-known poem, though the action does not relate directly to the substance of the poem itself. It is a drama of terror that offers a replay in the second part of the earlier action with a different time rhythm. The work was somewhat perplexing to the critics who felt that it aspired to a more important metaphysical comment than could possibly be inherent in the dramatic situation. Ruiz Ramón does not fault the interesting construction of the play but he does find a serious defect in Sastre's unsuccessful attempt to give transcendental importance to calculated mystery.[46] *The Raven* cannot be considered one of Sastre's more successful accomplishments; but, unfortunately, it was this lesser effort rather than one of his more compelling revolutionary works that audiences were permitted to see in 1957.

Sastre's adaptation of *Medea* was produced in 1958, but it was not until January, 1960, when *La cornada* (Death Thrust) was staged that he was again represented in the Madrid theater listings by an original work. *Death Thrust* lasted only fifty performances, but it is clearly one of the best of the Sastre plays that have been authorized to be performed in Spain. It is written in a different form from *Condemned Squad* or *The Gag*. It contains a prologue (set in the infirmary of a bullring), two relatively short acts which take place in a hotel suite, and an epilogue which is set in a tavern and which requires no specifically realistic decor. Sounds such as falling rain, thunder, trumpet calls, ovations, and the cries of terror from the arena are integral parts of the presentation. The action centers on the plight of the bullfighter José Alba and the insensitivity of his greedy manager Marcos. The prologue presents the death of Alba; and the events leading up to his fatal goring are told in flashback in the two central acts. Alba had lost his courage on the day of an important *corrida*; Marcos had insisted that he comply with his contract; and to avoid the fight, the bullfighter stabbed himself in the stomach. The wound is treated and Alba enters the ring—in spite of the unfavorable weather—to meet his death. In the epilogue, Marcos is seeking a new protégé to replace Alba. He offers to make a great celebrity of a young man named Rafael, but the latter refuses to be added to the list of victims. At the very end of the play, an ex-bullfighter whom Marcos had sponsored years before enters a café in rags to beg. He extends his hand to Marcos without even being recognized by his former manager. The beggar then turns to the audience to reveal his mutilated face as the sound of the rain continues.

In his *autocrítica* for *Death Thrust*, Sastre explained his own reasons for writing the drama:

I have tried to make a drama of an almost anthropophagic relationship—something like a present-day treatment of the myth of Saturn: a myth I find very much present in this society—and a little-known type of Spanish tragedy has been the result. Thus I fulfill an old literary dream: to treat the theme of bullfighting, so rich in meaning in Spain. It isn't that I'm a partisan of a nationalistic literature, . . . but neither do I subscribe to an uprooted cosmopolitanism; I try to operate . . . on a terrain distant from these two literary aberrations; although this time the theme may seem to be more Spanish than other times. . . . I'm dealing with reality . . . but through invented characters and a situation that is far from photographic. [47]

Death Thrust does not offer concessions to popular taste nor to those who resent a negative depiction of the exploitation that prevails while "selling" the talents of a bullfighter. The play is not social drama in the widest sense but rather a tragedy with social implications deriving from one man's struggle against a personal injustice that is far from unique. Ruiz Ramón ranks the play among Sastre's most important efforts,[48] and Farris Anderson's admiration for the work is clear in his detailed analysis.[49]

En la red (In the Net) was performed in 1961 by the *Grupo de teatro Realista ("Realistic Theater Group")* which had been organized by Sastre and his close associate Jose María de Quinto. The play dealt with the then-timely subject of the Algerian drive for independence from France, presenting the theme of responsibility felt within a small circle of French supporters of the Algerian cause. Because of the political implications of the work, performances outside of Madrid were not permitted (an example of the unpredictable nature of censorial prohibitions that have plagued Sastre). Also in 1961, Sastre and José María de Quinto composed and distributed a strong manifesto entitled *"Documento sobre el teatro español"* (Document on the Spanish Theater) which demanded the abolishment of censorship and denounced its effects on creativity as a cultural calamity for Spain.

Although *Asalto nocturno* (Nocturnal Assault)—written in 1959—was staged by an experimental group in Barcelona in 1965, only one original play by Sastre has had a major Madrid production in the past twelve years. *Oficio de tinieblas* (Office of Darkness) opened on February 8, 1967 (five years after its completion) to a mixed critical reception and only modest public interest. The work represented a dramatic style that Sastre has since abandoned in favor of what Anderson calls "post-Brechtian" principles. Dealing with the predicament of a man falsely accused of murdering a young woman, it is essentially a mystery with characters drawn from a segment of Madrid's contemporary *dolce vita*. Written in three acts, it is a rather conventional play in its structure, though the dialogue, according to the playwright, represents an attempt at an expansion of the language used in his earlier dramas, a liberation from the didactic speech that had frequently been apparent in his writing.[50]

Anderson has classified Sastre's total theater as either "dramas of frustration" or "dramas of possibility."[51] In the first category he places seven plays: *Ha sonado la muerte* (Death Has Sounded), *Uranium 235*, *Cargamento de sueños* (Cargo of Dreams, 1946); *Comedia sonámbula* (Sleepwalker's Comedy, 1947); *Ana Kleiber*, *The Blood of God* (1955); and *The Raven* (1956). In these works we find recurring situations, which do not deal with broad social issues, in which individuals are helpless in the face of circumstances. The remainder of the playwright's work—although demonstrating varied aesthetic and technical approaches—can be placed in the second grouping: *Prólogo patético* (Pathetic Prologue), *El cubo de basura* (The Garbage Pail, 1951); *Condemned Squad, Community Bread* (1953); *The Red Earth* (1954); *Sad are the Eyes of William Tell, Death in the Neighborhood* (1955); *In the Net, Nocturnal Assault, Death Thrust* (1959); *Office of Darkness* (1962); and his most recent works (all unpublished), *La sangre y las cenizas* (The Blood and the Ashes, 1965), *La taberna fantástica* (The Fantastic Tavern, 1966) *El banquete* (The Banquet, 1967), *Crónicas romanas* (Roman Chronicles, 1968). In these plays the central characters succeed in facing their predicaments and in some way altering their conditions. As Anderson points out, the situations of the characters—generally involving a wider social scheme—are not beyond their understanding, and the acts they commit for their own personal redemption have social significance.[52]

Although all of Sastre's early unperformed plays have been published and can at least be read and discussed, the major works of recent years exist only in manuscript form. Since 1965, the playwright has eschewed Aristotelian dramatic principles in favor of an admittedly Brechtian theater in which alienation or distanciación are the dramatic aims. *The Banquet* and *The Fantastic Tavern* are contemporary in setting and theme. The former shows some similiarity to *Death Thrust* in its treatment of the exploitation of celebrities. The action takes place in Málaga during the filming of a motion picture and deals with the discovery and causes of the death of an actress who has committed suicide after being raped during the filming of a pornographic scene. *The Fantastic Tavern* takes place in a tavern in a working-class district of Madrid and is concerned with the nomadic *quinquilleros* (roughly, "tinkers") who have failed to achieve social integration and live in miserable conditions while following their own special life style.

Roman Chronicles and *The Blood and the Ashes* both have historical settings and represent a move toward revolutionary theater based on epic principles. The first deals with the Roman siege of the Spanish city of Numancia (the subject of a play by Cervantes in the sixteenth century) and relates events of the distant past to contemporary imperialism. The play has twenty-six scenes, and the dialogue contains frequent allusions indicating a modern antiimperialist stance. The central character of *The Blood and the Ashes* is the unorthodox Spanish theologian and physician Miguel Servet, who was burned at the stake by the Calvinists in Geneva in 1553. Anderson summarizes the characteristics of all of the "epic" plays of Sastre as: looseness of structure; narrative elements (asides and speeches delivered directly to the audience); fusion of reality and pretense; unnerving sound, light, and visual effects; stylistic variety or incongruity; and the familiar presented in a strange light (for example, by suggesting mythic figures in his characters).[53]

Sastre has written extensively on the nature of theater and his own creative aims (not always fulfilled in his plays), and he has launched attacks against what he considers to be noncommitted theater among many of his contemporaries. His most important statements have been collected in *Drama y sociedad* (Drama and Society) (Taurus, 1956) and *Anatomía del realismo* (Anatomy of Realism) (Seix Barral, 1965). A more recent work, *La revolución y la crítica de la cultura* (Revolution and the Criticism of Culture) was published by Grijalbo (Barcelona) in 1970. Because of problems in achieving productions of his plays in Spain and the relatively minor interest in staging them in translation, Sastre continues to find himself an outsider among important creators of world theater. As in the case of Buero-Vallejo, the English-speaking theatrical establishment and those dedicated to experimental theater have given him only scant recognition to date.[54]

IV *Alfonso Paso*

Alfonso Paso Gil (b. 1926), like Mihura, has lived from childhood in intimate contact with the theatrical life of Madrid. His father was the popular and respected Andalusian playwright Antonio Paso Cano, and his mother the actress Juana Gil Andrés. From the age of five he went with his father to rehearsals and performances, and association with actors, directors, and writers was a normal part of his existence. A friend from childhood was Alfonso Sastre with whom he worked in close cooperation in experimental theater during their university days. In 1952, Paso

married Evangelina Jardiel,[55] daughter of one of Spain's most
original twentieth-century dramatists. In spite of his favorable
connections, Paso's early days as a playwright were difficult. He
did not earn income sufficient to provide more than the barest
necessities of life. In the late 1950's he began to enjoy
extraordinary popularity with the theater public. Although not all
of his works have been box office successes or had lengthy runs,
at one time or another as many as five of his comedies and
mysteries have been playing simultaneously in Madrid.

Paso has proved to be the most productive theatrical writer of
the postwar Spanish theater. Dramatic fecundity is hardly new in
Spain, but any dramatist who completes more than a hundred
and twenty-five works in a period of two decades is a rare
individual regardless of the degree of literary importance of his
efforts. Prolificness does not necessarily indicate routine or
mediocre results, and Paso's contribution to the Spanish stage is
such that it cannot be ignored. He is an eclectic writer at best,
admitting influences ranging from his late father-in-law Jardiel
Poncela to Tennessee Williams. Like several other Spanish
dramatists active during the past twenty years, he has varied his
product—offering comedies (serious, light, poetical, satirical),
mysteries (both straight suspense and those with elements of
parody), works of dark humor, serious dramas, and historical
plays which demonstrate a personal view and interpretation of
major figures of the past. Although he has not followed the
single-minded course of the controversial Sastre, Paso has
frequently demonstrated his awareness of the staleness of writing
and production that prevailed during his early career. As a man
of the theater, he also noted the antiquated staging facilities as
well as the conservatism of the theatergoing public. He has
spoken frankly about the inhibiting censorial prohibitions and of
the sometimes amusing ways in which he has circumvented
them. But for the most part he has devoted himself to providing
a steady theatrical fare of a traditional type that more often than
not must be treated as ephemeral entertainment. Nevertheless,
an examination of almost any Paso play selected at random would
provide some evidence of the theatrical know-how of the
playwright and even of his undeniably subtle intelligence.

Paso's careful application of his talent in the creation of popular
comedy can be illustrated by *Cosas de papá y mamá*

(Old-Fashioned Notions, 1960) which enjoyed a run of some six hundred performances (far more than those achieved by any of his more serious efforts). By reversing the traditional situation of parental opposition to the marriage of their children and placing a son and a daughter in the position of opposing the autumnal union of their respective parents, the playwright creates a dramatic conflict for *Old-Fashioned Notions* that is calculated to appeal to an older (and more loyal) theater public. He effectively disguises the basically conventional structure of his play by the introduction of a narrator (Dr. Bolt), who makes his first entrance from the audience to introduce in "Prologue One" his theory that death is precipitated by despair or by a loss of one's purpose in life and that "living represents a tremendous effort of the will." In the following scene—whimsically called "Prologue Two" but really the first act by the usual dramatic measurements—the principal characters are introduced in a farcical meeting in Dr. Bolt's office. A young woman named Luisa and her ailing mother Elena, who are waiting for a consultation, are soon joined by Julio and his hypochondriacal father Leandro. The dramatist carefully informs his audience that both parents are still in their forties—even though their dejected appearances at this point do not support the fact—and fully susceptible to sexual attraction, for later the mother pretends a pregnancy that is ultimately a reality in order to overcome her daughter's intransigence. Paso startles us at the end of "Prologue Two" with a second "physician" who is planted in the audience to initiate a debate with Bolt on the virtues of penicillin. But after the two prologues, the play settles into a conventional format that is abandoned only momentarily when Bolt continues his comments to the audience.

Paso is, of course, fully aware that the transformation of aging characters into a second youth by romance touches the illusions of his public. But he adds sufficient pathos before the happy ending to remind us that his theme has its tragic as well as its farcical possibilities. *Old-Fashioned Notions* also has its measure of satire (less biting than we find in some of the playwright's comic works) and its flashes of comic inspiration. Only a genuine humorist could measure so properly the amount of humor that can be squeezed from Elena's allergic reaction to Leandro's cologne or from the enamored woman's attempt to corroborate Leandro's invented tale of how he seduced her. Leandro's redecorating of his living room totally in green introduces an element of the absurd and bespeaks the continuing influence of Jardiel Poncela in Paso's theater.

Although *Old-Fashioned Notions* is the type of play certain to trigger the ire of the spokesmen for committed theater, an attack on such a comedy because of its lack of transcendental content would be a waste of ammunition. At the time of its premiere, the leading critics Adolfo Prego and Alfredo Marquerie both accepted the play for what it is: brisk, farcical entertainment. Marquerie noted numerous influences that could be detected in the work (Thornton Wilder, Gómez de la Serna, the Quintero brothers, Félicien Marceau, and others) but recommended that it not be considered a piece of second-hand theater since the stamp of Paso himself was unmistakable throughout the comedy.[56]

One of the better examples of Paso's suspense drama is *Juicio contra un sinvergüenza* (The Trial of a Scoundrel, 1958), a moralistic play that reveals certain pretensions to social significance but which is in essence a variation of the "courtroom" play in which the innocence of a suspected or accused character is determined by the astute questioning of a perceptive lawyer or prosecutor. The difference in this case is that the accused himself stages his defense in his own house through a clever manipulation of his accusers. Juan Esquín, a former dignitary in a British ministry office, confronts a group of his former associates following his dismissal from his post because of reported extramarital affairs and misuse of government funds. Now separated from his wife, Laura, he elects to interrupt one of her parties to prove his innocence—or, more specifically, the guilt of those closest to him. He suggests a *juego* ("game") that will be more diverting than the usual bridge or poker game in which these dull people fill the gaps of their lives. The new game turns out to be a trial with witnesses and a jury (represented by an outspoken servant girl).

Paso himself has described this play as "an outcry in two acts" and has asserted that it is the first Spanish play that could be considered in the line of "angry theater" written in England by John Osborne and others.[57] But the substance of *The Trial of a Scoundrel* hardly justifies the playwright's inclusion among the "angry young men." As in many of his less ambitious efforts, Paso seems intent on amazing the audience with his capacity for putting together a jigsaw of loose pieces of evidence. In spite of the stated indictment of corruption in government circles, it is difficult to accept this play as a work of any profound social or moral significance. The characters themselves are only ciphers, and the exposure of the plot against the protagonist provides little more than relief from the suspense cleverly built up over a period of some two hours.

Paso takes his writing seriously and stands on his own judgments of the relative merits of his plays rather than accepting the opinions of others. And he is, to be sure, hardly modest in instances where he considers his achievement to be solid. Among the serious dramas of the playwright, *Los pobrecitos* (The Poor Sad People, 1957) is one of the most highly regarded—though Paso himself has said that it is "a good tragicomedy plagued with defects."[58] Like López Rubio's *Alberto*, the play is set in a Madrid *pensión,* and the natures of a varied group of boarders are laid bare in the course of the three acts. But while *Alberto* is essentially a study of human capacity for subscribing to illusion, with elements of social satire, *The Poor Sad People* deals more directly with the dire financial plight of the characters and with the effects of poverty on their lives. One of the group (Carlos) is an unsuccessful playwright; another (Lorencito) is deformed and his mother seeks money for an operation that she hopes will alleviate his condition. All of the boarders are at the mercy of the greedy landlady (Doña Clara). Suddenly cash is sent to each of the needy in envelopes. They speculate on its origin; but eventually it turns out that Leonor, an imaginative and quixotic spinster, has taken the funds from a bank simply by picking them up when the teller was distracted. Although there are some passages of overblown dialogue in the play, and the denouement seems contrived, *The Poor Sad People* is undeniably an engaging and sometimes affecting piece of dramatic writing. It is not, however, one of the major works of its time nor is it profoundly involved in the social injustices that have created the desperation and frustration that darken the lives of the characters.

Garcia Pavón considers *La boda de la chica* (The Daughter's Marriage, 1960) to be a somewhat more successful attempt at social commentary—though not a drama that provokes any desire to alter the *status quo.*[59] The use of parallel actions onstage provides a more imaginative dramatic situation than that of *The*

Poor Sad People. In this drama the unhappiness of both the struggling poor and the rich business class is considered. The poor family has the hope of bettering its situation through the marriage of their daughter (Antonia) to an engineer. When the expected suitor does not appear to meet the family, the parents are spared total humiliation through a deception contrived by their son who persuades a friend to impersonate the engineer. In the wealthy family, tradition and self-interest dictate that the father oppose the romance of his daughter (Marisol) with a young man of the working class. The play ends with an implied happy solution for both young women, and the possible tragic results for one or the other are avoided. Paso has created a complex and effective dramatic structure for this work; and like a number of other writers of the postwar theater, he has utilized the device of theater-within-theater as a carefully integrated part of the action. In spite of an ending that most would consider a concession to the public, *The Daughter's Marriage* was not a great box office success and closed before it achieved a hundred performances.

In 1956 Paso offered his first play on a historical theme. *Catalina no es formal* (Catharine is Not a Serious Girl) deals with the young Catharine of Anhalt-Zerbst who went to Russia to marry the heir to the throne and later came to be known as Catharine the Great. Its central theme is the corruption of innocence as personal power increases. The action covers the period from Catharine's arrival in Russia to the revolution which brought her to power. Like the two historical plays that have followed, it makes no attempt at literal historical realism—although certain scenes are based on factual material. The anachronisms throughout the play are, of course, intentional and represent the playwright's desire to show the possibilities for recurrence (or even the inevitability) of his illustrative dramatic situation.

Paso's next historical work, *Preguntan por Julio César* (Call for Julius Casesar, 1960), deserves mention if only for its outlandish view of one of history's most famous encounters between man and woman. There is little danger that Paso's Caesar, Cleopatra, and Antony will erase memories of these personages as imagined by Shakespeare in his Roman plays or by Shaw. Cleopatra is a caricature—skinny as a pencil, stoop-shouldered, and padded into some resemblance of her reported allure. In matters of politics and history she is an utter ninny. When she sits she has a problem with her false hips. Inevitably one recalls the television parodies of the comedienne Imogene Coca, for the opening scene of the play resembles nothing so much as a skit from "The Show of Shows." Antony is conceited in the broadest sense; Caesar is short and myopic, with little of the bearing of a great leader; and his dialogue is more Wildean than Shakespearian. At the end of the first act, he and Cleopatra sit playing a children's game (throwing rocks into a circle). Caesar's victory in the game suggests, to be sure, Rome's ultimate triumph.

In the third act the dialogue becomes more serious. Caesar's epilepsy is discussed and there is an extraordinarily shrewd scene in which Caesar tricks his opponents into drinking their own poison. As a kind of burlesque of history, *Call for Julius Caesar* is frequently quite funny; in its most memorable scene it is engrossingly clever; but it is never very profound in spite of an obvious attempt at significant commentary on political manipulation. In its totality it is an unsuccessful effort to reinterpret history by challenging the traditional concepts of characters of near-mythic nature and at the same time retain the essence of their momentous encounter.

The playwright's third and most important historical drama opened in Madrid on September 6, 1969. *Nerón-Paso*—short for the longest title in the annals of Spanish theater: *Persecución de los cristianos por el emperador Nerón, según la idea y concepto que del hecho tiene el autor español Alfonso Paso* (Persecution of the Christians by the Emperor Nero, according to the Idea and Concept that the Spanish Author Alfonso Paso Has of the Events)[60]—follows the line of the two earlier works in its aim to demythify historical characters, but its distinctive form and serious realization elevate the work above its predecessors—at least in terms of literary values. Paso makes extensive use of a *Relator* ("Commentator") in modern dress who contributes to the intended alienation and relates the events to more recent happenings (such as the Communist Revolution in Russia).[61] The Commentator's speeches are notably long—a defect of the play in that they consume virtually as much time as the actions of the characters themselves.

In a preface to *Nero-Paso*, the author has carefully documented the extensive research he did on the events of the period he has treated. He seeks to destroy the "myth" of Nero's cruelty by showing him as a relatively sensitive man (and *relatively* less cruel than others) who is caught in a web of intrigue and in a revolt that he would prefer to wish away. The play is divided into six episodes that cover a period of four years, with interspersed speeches by the Commentator. The opening episode presents the arrival of Nero to Rome *after* the city has begun burning. In the succeeding episodes we see the confrontation of the emperor and Siano, the Christian rebel whose calls to violence do not correspond to his professed religion, and the relationship of Nero to Poppea, the poet Lucan, and the homosexual philosopher Seneca (among other characters). In the fifth episode, a scene of extreme brutality is enacted onstage when Poppea executes a Jewish girl (Eunosia) by inserting a heated iron into her vitals. In the final section, Nero commits suicide with the help of the loyal Acté. The decadence of Roman society and the homosexuality and lesbianism of specific characters is discussed frankly and extendedly in the dialogue but they remain things talked about rather than practiced in any pronounced way in the stage action.

The critic for *A B C* showed a respectful attitude toward the production of *Nero-Paso* (and toward Paso's performance of the title role) but he questioned the playwright's choice of Nero as a hero—or antihero—to serve as a paradigm for contemporary situations.[62] Paso himself considers the play to be his most important achievement and has expressed confidence that it will endure as a major contribution to world theater.[63] Like most of Paso's work, *Nero-Paso* betrays the author's debt to other dramatists. Certainly influences of Giraudoux's *Judith* and *La guerre de Troie n'aura pas lieu* can be detected; and a Brechtian narrator is a major feature of the drama. The most original aspect—and one that is supported well by the playwright in his dialogue—is the reinterpretation of Nero as a historical personage. He is seen as a man who could not comprehend the upheavals of his time; his role as a monster was inevitable given the confluence of events. Seneca states this view to Nero early in the play and cautions him against actions he cannot totally avoid:

SENECA. It's inevitable, Nero. The chronicles will say that I was a philosopher and you a monster. That's already decreed. I'm not a bother to Christianity. Quite the contrary. But you are. They need to be persecuted by somebody. You should be careful not to persecute them. That's my advice.[64]

Paso has not been indifferent to the need to produce a more committed theater in Spain, but he cannot see this renovation being achieved through a total repudiation of the existing theatrical habits and institutions. Rather, he has chosen to make a "pact" with the public and to seek to achieve a type of evolution from within. Such a view has naturally had its outspoken critics, and much of Paso's writing can be used to support those who attack him as a fabricator of entertainments. Certainly the evidence that he has actually contributed to the evolution of Spain's theater is scant; more works on the level of *Nero-Paso*, *The Daughter's Marriage*, or the imaginative comedy *En el Escorial, cariño mío* (At El Escorial, My Dear, 1968) will be required to alter to any appreciable degree the image that now exists of Alfonso Paso's theater.

CHAPTER 4

The Second Group of
Postwar Dramatists

1 Dramatists of Social Protest

CARLOS Muñiz, Ricardo Rodríguez Buded, and Lauro Olmo have been the leading representatives of an identifiable theater of social protest which owes a debt to the example of Buero-Vallejo's *Story of a Stairway* and Sastre's call for a more socially committed drama as well as to influences from outside Spain. In spite of the relatively small number of their works that were actually staged, the role of these playwrights in the development of serious peninsular theater in the late 1950's and early 1960's was an important one.

Telarañas (Cobwebs), the first play of Carlos Muñiz Higuera (b. 1927), received an overwhelmingly negative response from the Madrid critics when it was produced in 1955. Later the same year, the author won a literary prize for *El grillo* (The Cricket), which was finally staged in 1957. *The Cricket*, called "a strident concerto in two acts and an epilogue" by the author, is a terse, realistic drama dealing with the financial dilemma of an office worker. Although the reception of the work was less than enthusiastic, the prominent theater critic Pérez Minik has proclaimed *The Cricket* to be a major contribution to social theater worthy of consideration beside *Death of a Salesman* or *Look Back in Anger*.[1] *El precio de los sueños* (The Price of Dreams), another realistic work concerned with the difficulties of reconciling financial actualities with social aspirations, was awarded the Carlos Arniches Drama Prize in 1959. Muñiz then elected a frankly antinaturalistic, expressionistic form for his next play, *El tintero* (The Inkwell, 1961). The playwright labeled this searing indictment of a bureaucracy drained of even the vestiges of human concern a "farce in two parts and a fantasy." However, "tragic farce" would perhaps be a more apt description of the story of the pathetic and helpless antihero Crock who is ultimately the victim of a society that is moved only by financial considerations, while openingly scorning the man who seeks to retain some ties with his natural environment. In the description of the setting, Muñiz notes: "The action occurs in a place where there are men, where money exists, where ambition overrules their hearts, where it doesn't matter if a man dies. Our own time. Or hundreds of years ago. Or within a hundred years, if no remedy is effected."[2]

Crock is an underpaid office worker who returns to his village each weekend to visit his wife and children. But the mental stress of working under the relentless surveillance of an excessively organized bureaucracy and the physical strain of the long trip by bicycle leave him too exhausted to make love with his wife. She, in turn, demonstrates her impatience and frustration by turning to a robust school teacher for physical gratification. Crock's only source of sympathy is a character called *"El Amigo"* (The Friend) who accompanies him (to no avail) in his search for a home for his family in the city. Without a down payment and appropriate references from his employer, Crock is unable to alter his deplorable existence in the slightest. He finds himself a cuckold, despised by his wife, and held in contempt by his superiors. In a final effort to provide funds to maintain his family, he resorts to selling his body to a medical school. Finally he meets death under the wheels of a passing train. In an epilogue—which to some might seem a superfluous addition to the play—Crock is reunited with The Friend in the other world. However, this scene is in no way a sentimental concession to the public. Rather than receiving any conventional rewards for good intentions, Crock and The Friend hear the fading sound of the death-dealing train replaced by the sounds of the sea,[3] indicating their reunion with the earth to which they had been denied communion by a corrupt system. The final section of dialogue has its own poetic overtones:

> CROCK. . . . The moon is rising! What is that?
> THE FRIEND. The passenger train.
> CROCK. What train?
> THE FRIEND. Any train. What difference does it make?
> CROCK. That's true! What difference does it make! Do you want to take a walk?

THE FRIEND. Sure. Which way?
CROCK. It's all the same. We're not in a hurry any more. (*They look at each other. There is a pause, and they begin to laugh. Their laughter grows louder to the point of raucousness. We begin to hear the sound of the waves.*)

CROCK. What is that?
THE FRIEND. It sounds like the sea.
CROCK. The sea.[4]

It seems likely that *The Inkwell* had some influence on Calvo-Sotelo's *The Innocent One* (written in 1968;). Both works deal in an antirealistic format with individuals who are at odds with the system under which they are forced to exist. Yet the two plays are quite distinct because of an essential difference in the natures of the two antiheroes. Crock is a Kafkaesque creation, the victim of an organization that permits no escape in life; Dominico Loredo y Valderrama is victim of his own obstinate candor, and at one point or another could conceivably have altered his course. In terms of dramatic inventiveness Calvo-Sotelo's play has a slight edge over *The Inkwell*; but by pulling Dominico back from the wheels of the subway at the last moment, what had seemed inevitable is avoided by the contrived intervention of another character and the import of the drama is diluted. Muñiz's play, on the other hand, is an authentic tragicomedy—touched by the darkest kind of humor—which follows an unswerving line toward the tragic downfall of the central character.

García Pavón has noted that the establishment critics correctly pointed out the echoes of Chaplin, Kafka, and even Brecht in *The Inkwell*, while Sastre and Daniel Sueiro wrote articles linking the expressionism of the play with Quevedo's *Buscón* and other examples of the picaresque novel.[5] Obviously, the theme of hunger is one that has its roots in the classical literature of Spain, but García Pavón does not accept Muñiz's drama as a direct descendant of Quevedo's novel in concept and realization. If the play calls to mind dramatic works from other countries (for example, *The Adding Machine* of Elmer Rice), it does not seem in any sense imitative or excessively derivative. Although the problem treated is recognized in many places other than Spain, Muñiz's approach is decidedly that of a Hispanic writer who is capable of suggesting the subtle but real peculiarities of Spanish bureaucracy and their effects on a simple man who has lived close to the earth before finding himself deprived of even the most modest symbols of nature. He is humiliated by his wife's infidelity—a humiliation that deprives him of his right to manhood in the eyes of a Mediterranean society that reserves a special contempt for the cuckold. In its totality, *The Inkwell* is a powerful work of theater and one that inspires a sense of urgency to stem the power of an automated organization to negate all humanistic concerns.

Las viejas difíciles (The Difficult Old Ladies, 1966) follows the expressionistic line of *The Inkwell*. Like the characters of Muñiz's earlier works, the principal figures (Antonio and Julita) are frustrated by an unthinking establishment in the consummation of their sincere love for each other. After years of loyal devotion they are arrested for kissing publicly in a park. They are persecuted by the "Association of Honorable Ladies" who are in this work the representatives of the dehumanized. *Un solo de saxofón* (A Saxophone Solo, 1965), a one-act play, also deals with society's relentless persecution of its victims.

Little biographical material on Ricardo Rodríguez Buded (192-) has been published. His first play, *Un hombre duerme* (A Man is Sleeping), was winner of the Valle-Inclán Prize in 1959 and was performed in May, 1960. It clearly demonstrated the author's firm dedication to theater of social concern. Fundamentally realistic in concept but with touches of the absurd, the work treats the predicament of a family whose members meet weekly in a café because the father cannot obtain sufficient income to provide an appropriate home. As in several of Carlos Muñiz's plays, the question of inequities in the distribution of wealth underlies the action. *La madriguera* (The Lair), staged in December, 1960, is a more complex and less static effort which deals with a group of the underprivileged who are compelled to live in the shabby rented rooms of a depressing tenement. Forced proximity breeds tensions, conflicts, and a sense of desperation that color the lives of the characters. In his *autocrítica*, the playwright notes that his intention was not to allow any single character to assume the dimensions of a protagonist. As in Buero's *Story of a Stairway*, the physical setting is the unifying element in the drama. Rodríguez Buded's device of showing simultaneously the lives of more than one family had, of course, already been employed in *Story of a Stairway* (where the action takes place outside the four apartments) and in Paso's *The Daughter's Marriage* (where parallel actions are maintained). Ruiz Ramón sees the "small hell" of the characters of *The Lair* as a variation of the hell of Sartre's *No Exit* but conceived as a denunciation in a social sense of the prevailing conditions that permit such inescapable spiritual degradation.[6]

The playwright's third work, *El charlatán* (The Charlatan) was first performed on February 23, 1962, before a sympathetic opening night audience, but it did not prove to be financially successful. Again Rodríguez Buded followed a line of realism, presenting literal events with a minimum of expository dialogue. However, the psychological penetration is deeper than in the two plays that preceded it. At the time of the premiere, Torrente Ballester expressed admiration for *The Charlatan* but added reservations about the ultimate development of the final act.[7] But his review, like those of other critics, only skimmed the surface of this complex and artistically conceived social drama touched with dark humor. Later, Ruiz Ramón, in his quite brief comments on the play, described *The Charlatan* as Rodríguez Buded's "most ambiguous" play.[8] Whatever the reasons for a degree of perplexity that can be sensed in the critical commentaries, the work ranks among the better Spanish dramas of the 1960's and suggests the potential of its author more forcefully than his earlier efforts. The action is centered on the extraordinarily successful participation of Luisa, a high-strung woman of thirty-five, in radio contests conducted by telephone. She finds herself alienated from her avaricious family and pretends illness as a kind of protest or retaliation. In a double deceit, the parents pretend to think the girl is ill even though the doctors have told them that she has been cured of an earlier affliction. The "charlatan" of the play is the picaresque Adolfo, an artist-turned-house painter who is brought to the apartment to redecorate the rooms that have been collecting grime for decades. Amusingly, the family has chosen battleship gray for the new color—and the playwright leaves no doubt that color symbolism is an intended part of his dramatic scheme. Adolfo, the nonconformist, tells the mother: "You resist colors, light frightens you."[9] Adolfo is a goad for all the other characters. He antagonizes Luisa's dull fiancé César, whose idea of excitement is watching soccer games through binoculars from the apartment roof; he also penetrates the façades of the father and of the mother, with her Galdosian obsession for money and material gain. But it is with Luisa that his influence is most profound. He inspires in her a desire to escape her stifling, colorless existence, but finally he must tell her that he does not love her and that he cannot guarantee the realization of the very dreams he has helped nurture in her. Like some of Buero's female characters, Luisa achieves a meaningful but painful inner victory. She abandons her illusion of a life of adventure with Adolfo and indicates that she will terminate her prolonged engagement to César by marriage.

The high point for the contemporary theater of social concern in Spain came in 1962 with the production of Lauro Olmo's *La camisa* (The Shirt). Olmo (b. 1927) had been recognized as a promising but marginal poet and novelist for several years before the premiere of *The Shirt* brought him acclaim as a playwright. This first play received an array of drama awards and also caught the interest of the public. The popular success of the work was due in part to its timely theme: the emigration of the unemployed of Spain to the more industrialized areas of western Europe (particularly West Germany) to achieve a higher standard of living. The principal characters of *The Shirt* live in a *chabola* ("shanty") on the outskirts of Madrid. Juan, the head of an impoverished family, is struggling to provide for his wife (Lola) and his children, but he refuses to follow the example of his friends who are leaving for Germany to seek work. The title of the play refers to the white shirt that Lola purchases (in vain) for her husband so that he can apply for a job in respectable attire. Eventually, Lola herself decides to leave Spain with the funds her mother had saved for her funeral.

The Shirt is a vivid and moving account of the existence of an element of Spanish society, with all the natural color and bluntness of the speech of the semieducated captured in the dialogue. Although distinctly tragic in tone, the play is not lacking in lighter *costumbrista* elements (frequently earthy) that provide balance in the playwright's realistic and credible dramatic situations. With *English spoken*[10] (1968), Olmo again presented a theme that was both timely and significant to an understanding of the contemporary fabric of Spanish society. In this instance it was the return of Spaniards who have lived for a period abroad. The positive as well as the negative influence of this experience is considered, but it is the negative that stands out. *English spoken* is a sincerely felt indictment of exploitation and the cynical adoption of non-Spanish mores. Unfortunately, the play lacks the tight structure and dramatic power that had characterized *The Shirt*.

II José Martín Recuerda

José Martín Recuerda was born in 1925 in Granada, the Andalusian city where García Lorca lived and died. In 1958 he gained public attention when *El teatrito de Don Ramón* (Don Ramón's Small Theater), his fourth play, was awarded the prestigious Lope de Vega Prize. However, his name was already familiar in theatrical circles because of his accomplishments as director of the *T.E.U. (Teatro español universitario)* of Granada. His first play, *La llanura* (The Plain) had been staged by his university group in 1954, and two other early works were subsequently performed. During the same period he was awarded a scholarship by the French government to study theater at the Sorbonne. Because of a criticized reading of his play *Las salvajes en Puente San Gil* (The Savages in Puente San Gil) in the Mediterranean city of Motril, he was removed from his teaching post in Granada in 1962. The playwright has lectured on Spanish drama in the United States and was a visiting professor at the University of Washington.

Don Ramón's Small Theater was not a great public success when it was produced in April, 1959; the critical reception was also less than enthusiastic. Nevertheless, this tragic and poetic depiction of destroyed hopes and illusions ranks closer in quality to Buero's *Story of a Stairway* than any other play to win the Lope de Vega Prize in the past two decades. (Significantly, in its published form the work is dedicated to Buero-Vallejo.) The "small theater" of the title is an attic with a makeshift stage where Don Ramón has staged modest theatricals for the pleasure of his friends over a period of some thirty years. It also symbolizes the very life and hopes of the man himself. When the play opens, Don Ramón is preparing for a performance of a miracle play adapted by his friend Don Anacleto from "*El milagro de Teófilo*" by the medieval poet Berceo. A conspicuous object in the "theater" is a dilapidated antique chair that has been provided for the expected attendance of the local archbishop. This chair, with broken springs and faded upholstery, stands throughout the play as a vivid symbol of the frustrated expectations of the characters, for the prelate never appears.

Don Ramón is nervous about his own role of Teófilo. He explains that he would have been a better actor if he had been able to escape from the monotonous routine of a small-town office. For the aging people assuming roles and dressing in shabby costumes, Madrid holds an irresistible promise of success and beauty that they can never expect to encounter in their provincial town. Their words are reminiscent of the longing to return to Moscow expressed in Chekov's *Three Sisters:*

PURITA. Poor Don Anacleto. Why didn't he go off to Madrid? If he had gone in time, as we all advised him, he would be an honored writer today.
DON CEFERINO. I always told him: to Madrid, to Madrid. Life has slipped away from us without our ever knowing the joy of seeing Madrid.[11]

Ironically, some of those who did leave for the capital (the violinist Hilario and the "mad" Pola García) did not find true fame and are now forced to create fictions about their lives.

In addition to Don Ramón's most loyal following, the audience contains a group of disrespectful young women (*"las chicas de Morales"*) and an assortment of grotesque characters: the aged Doña María, The Woman With the Face of a Giraffe, and a hunchback. Some resemble bizarre figures from the *esperpentos* of Valle-Inclán. At the end of the first act, attention is focused on the empty chair as the assembly awaits the arrival of the archbishop. At the suggestion of Don Ramón they all kneel down with the conviction that the prelate will soon pass through the doorway and that his arrival will somehow alter their lives (in short, a miracle). It is a scene of extraordinary dramatic power and a clear demonstration of Martín Recuerda's unusual theatrical inventiveness.

The second act begins with the presentation of the play-within-the-play, but the performance is interrupted by the noisy behavior of the Morales girls. Doña Jorgina, one of the performers, steps out of character to scold the disruptors, while the older members of the audience express their disapproval. The play continues to disintegrate as the mockery grows. (If the scene calls to mind the memorable "concert scene" of Buero's *The Concert at Saint Ovide*, it should be remembered that Buero's play had not yet been written and that it was performed some three years after the premiere of *Don Ramón's Small Theater*.) The performance is a disaster; the audience leaves; the set is dismantled; and Don Ramón is left alone. Suddenly he realizes that he has failed to put out food for the stray dog "King" that he had adopted. The play ends as the old man pleads pathetically for the dog not to abandon him:

DON RAMON. My little theater like this . . . in this shape. (*He looks at the remains with a terrible desolation. He goes over to the curtain and caresses it. Suddenly he remembers something.*) No. It can't be. I forgot to feed the dog. (*He goes quickly to the door. First he calls softly, fearing to bother the people in the other apartments.*) King, King. What if he's gone? (*He calls again in a louder voice.*) King, King. Is it possible he's gone away? King . . . King, not you. Not you. Not you. Don't leave me, King. (*He covers his ears with his hands. He seems not to want to see or hear and sinks in a heap to the floor before the stage of his small theater.*) King isn't coming. He isn't coming. Don't leave me, King. Don't leave me.[12]

Strangely, the critic Alfredo Marqueríe found this play to be dramatically uneven and ineffective. He described the first act as being no more than the wait for a visitor who does not come. He found the presentation of the "miracle" in the second act simply boring—apparently missing the importance of waiting to the meaning of the play and the symbolic significance of the performance itself.[13] Ricardo Domenech later wrote that the work deserved better than the critical rejection it had received; but at the same time he did not view the play as a major accomplishment.[14] Given these negative reactions, one can only wonder about the appropriateness of the direction and quality of the performances of the production of the play. Ruiz Ramón calls *Don Ramón's Small Theater* "a beautiful and tender poem, sad and pathetic . . . a deeply felt elegy."[15] Even after repeated readings, it remains a moving and impressive creation, imbued with theatricalism of the kind that lends distinction to dramatic art.

The playwright has written that he decided to fight back after the unsuccessful production of the play and that in the future he would not create characters like Don Ramón and his friends who let themselves be overcome by their failures.[16] His next effort, *The Savages in Puente San Gil*, fulfilled that pledge; but, according to the playwright, it was mutilated in its 1963 Madrid production.[17] In its published form, the play is a forceful piece of dramatic writing that exemplifies a type of theater of rebellion in which a nonconforming character or group of characters are aroused to action by the hypocrisy-tainted forces of conservatism. The action takes place in a provincial theater where the cast of a varieties show is preparing to open against the organized resistance of a group of hypocritical citizens. Ultimately a violent confrontation occurs. *Savages* is a less cohesive play than *Don Ramón* but a fine work in its own right and it provides further evidence of Martín Recuerda's superior creative talents.

Como las secas cañas del camino (Like the Dry Stalks Along the Way, 1965)[18] is an impressive drama of an aging school teacher whose passion for one of her former students leads her to ostracism and dismissal. It reveals Martín Recuerda's debt to both Lorca and Valle-Inclán. The protagonist (Julita) is a more sensual version of Lorca's Doña Rosita, while many of the characters that surround her are grotesque or deformed. There are also suggestions of Tennessee Williams's Blanche Dubois in the character of Julita, though this may be purely coincidental. And one scene with her younger lover shows a striking similarity in mood to the scene between Blanche and the newspaper boy in Williams's *Streetcar Named Desire*. Martín Recuerda maintains that he follows a strict line of "Iberianism," but most of his plays have the power and universality to be viable beyond the Spanish mainland. Certainly he is one of the strongest talents of his generation.

III *Antonio Gala*

Antonio Gala Velasco achieved a major success with a serious drama at a younger age than any other postwar Spanish dramatist. Born in Córdoba in 1939, he was only twenty-seven when his *Los verdes campos del Edén* (The Green Fields of Eden) was produced in 1963.[19] The critical interest that accompanied the premiere of this first work by Gala approached that which Buero's *Story of a Stairway* had inspired in 1949. The play won for its author the Calderón de la Barca Prize, and the succeeding efforts by the young dramatist were awaited with more than ordinary anticipation (though some critics felt that they did not fulfill the promise of the first).

The principal scenes of this loosely structured drama take place in a cemetery crypt where several characters, who might be described as disinherited members of society, seek a temporary haven from conditions that have created in them an intense feeling of desperation or alienation. In the opening scene, Juan (an outsider and nonconformist whose home has been destroyed by war) arrives in a town to seek the tomb that his grandfather had bought to accomodate six bodies. Lacking sufficient money to rent a room, he takes up residence in the crypt. Ana, a woman grieving for the loss of a man who loved her but who was married to another appears in the cemetery; Manuel and María, a young couple who cannot find privacy to make love in the overcrowded family quarters where four people sleep in the same bedroom, find that the cemetery is the only place they can be alone. At the end of the first act, Juan invites Ana to remain with him. The main action of the second part of the play is a New Year's Eve celebration in the crypt. Ironically, some of the guests are prostitutes from a café where life offers less joy than a graveyard. Eventually the celebration is halted by the authorities and the door to the tomb is sealed.

Although *The Green Fields of Eden* could be considered a drama of social indictment, it is touched with poetic insight, and moments of tenderness stand out. Christian symbolism is an important element in the play. For example, one of the guards is startled by the sound of a cock crowing, recalling Peter's denial of Christ; a wounded dove is discovered in the crypt, suggesting the abuse of faith; and the final sealing of the tomb is probably intended to recall the sealing of Christ's tomb after the crucifixion. In spite of its somewhat disjointed form, *The Green Fields of Eden* is an admirable work which demonstrates that a strong sense of the poetical is not incompatible with harsh social commentary. Gala himself referred to the play as a story of redemption,[20] and this led to the application of the label "*teatro de redención*" to his work. Actually the playwright considers his theater to be very much a part of the renovative movement to which Muñiz, Olmo, and Martín Recuerda (writers a few years his senior) have made notable contributions.[21]

Gala's next performed play, *El sol en el hormiguero* (The Sun on the Ant Hill, 1966), placed unusual demands upon both actors and public. It is a reinterpretation of Gulliver's visit to the Lilliputians in which a conservative society under the control of an absolute monarch is seen in all its absurdities. The satire is masterful and in the spirit of Swift's novel. Gulliver is not actually seen by the audience and exists only as an enormous presence that is discussed, communicated with indirectly, and ultimately destroyed. The king declares this troublesome visitor to be nonexistent. When the decree proves ineffectual in dealing with the problem, he assembles military weapons to kill the giant, whose enormous decaying body threatens the health of the nation. *The Sun on the Ant Hill* is a complex work that is filled with subtleties of thought as well as oblique allusions, implications, and political satire. To be effective in performance a special style of acting and extraordinarily imaginative staging would be essential. But it is a rewarding play that must rank as one of the most original contributions to recent Spanish theater.

Noviembre y un poco de hierba (November and a Bit of Grass, 1967) offers a strange dramatic situation (but one quite similar to a real-life situation that was later publicized in Spain) in which a republican soldier spends some twenty-seven years in hiding without leaving the basement where he has taken refuge. His wife supplies him with food and gives him the desire to survive. But when amnesty is declared, he is unable to rejoin the society that had made him a fugitive. He is accidentally killed when his wife urges him to abandon his retreat. With *Los buenos días perdidos* (The Good Days Lost, 1972)—described as a "tragic farce"—Gala returned to a terrain closer to that of his first play. The action takes place in the nave of a parochial church which becomes the abode of a strange family. The dramatist's most recent work, *Anillos para una dama* (Rings for a Lady) opened in Madrid in September, 1973, and proved to be his greatest box office success.

Gala has cultivated genres other than drama, and his poetry and essays have added to his literary reputation. However, a series of routine television plays which he wrote in 1968 provided few indications of the dramatic talent that he has so ably demonstrated in his works for the stage.

IV *Jaime Salom*

Jaime Salom has the distinction of being the only Catalán to achieve major renown in the contemporary Spanish theater centered in Madrid. Son of a prominent Mallorcan ophthalmologist, he was born in Barcelona on Christmas Day, 1925. In 1949 he completed his medical studies at the University of Barcelona with the intention of following the specialization of his father. During his university days he had won a prize for a play that was never performed. In 1954 his *El mensaje* (The Message) was staged in Bilbao. Although it was a moralistic suspense play of no great originality or distinction constructed along the most conventional lines, *The Message* was favorably received and was eventually given a second production in Barcelona.

Salom's *Verde esmeralda* (Emerald Green), a mystery farce, had a Madrid premier in 1960. The playwright's first genuine success came the following year with *Culpables* (Guilty), a mystery drama that was well constructed but not of any exceptional depth or originality. Salom's early popularity was based on works that placed no unexpected demands on audiences. But he began to follow a policy (already established by Calvo-Sotelo, Paso, Pemán, and others) of alternating light entertainments with plays of more serious intent. In 1964 his *El baúl de los disfraces* (The Trunk of Disguises) demonstrated a capacity for more imaginative design and more subtle dramatic substance in a serious comedy dealing with the awakening of romantic interest at various stages of life and recurring loss of illusions. The play requires only three actors who appear in various guises as the action moves from present to past and back to present. Songs are incorporated into the action to give the play an intended "Music Hall" flavor.

La casa de las chivas (The House of the "Chivas," 1969) was the play that ensured Salom celebrity status among the Spanish playwrights of his time. This highly charged, melodramatic work which takes place in the vicinity of Barcelona during the civil war proved to be one of the most popular dramas in the history of the

Spanish theater and had a run of some thirteen hundred performances. As the author tells us in his *autocrítica*,[22] as well as at the end of the play itself, *The House of the "Chivas"* is based on actual events, though they have obviously been interpreted for dramatic purposes. What is surprising, even in the light of censorial restrictions, is the almost total lack of political opinion or the expression of attitudes dealing directly with the war to be found in the dialogue. It is principally concerned with the influence of a seminarian who is lodged with other republican adherents in the house of a man whose wife (known as "La Chiva") and eldest daughter have left him shamed by their sexual activities. A younger daughter, who is still technically innocent at the beginning of the play, allows herself to be seduced by a married soldier. *The House of the "Chivas"* does not represent Salom's best work, but its blunt language and frank approach to the human (if not political) passions generated by the war attracted the interest of more Spaniards than generally frequent live performances. Later, a motion picture version brought the work to an even wider audience.

A more interesting drama of higher artistic merit is *Los delfines* (The Heirs Apparent) which had its premiere in Barcelona on January 31, 1969, and opened in Madrid the following October. In this prize-winning work, the playwright has attempted a significant dramatic statement about the conflict between generations in our own time as illustrated by the dissolution of a wealthy Barcelona family. The older generation is represented by an aristocratic industrialist, whose approach to business is that of an absolute dictator, surrounded by a few carefully chosen advisors who echo his ideas. On his eightieth birthday, he collapses and dies as guests are about to arrive for a celebration. His son Fernando (the "Dauphin" or "heir apparent," as the matriarch of the family perfers to call him) has no skill for organization and turns to the son (Raúl) of an old employee who has learned management techniques in the United States. Raúl suggests that the business be incorporated and that part of the stock be distributed among the workers. The widowed Doña Carolina is determined to prevent change. Thwarted by her unbending will and disillusioned by the unfaithfulness of his mistress, Fernando commits suicide, leaving a detailed written statement. Doña Carolina attempts to persuade Fernando's young son Fere to reassert a one-man rule in spite of the strikes and opposition of the workers. Fere refuses to become involved with the business and indicates his contempt for the self-made aristocracy into which he has been born. *The Heirs Apparent* may be less profound that the playwright intended, but it is an engrossing play that sustains Salom's claim to serious consideration among contemporary dramatists. Its inventive form, in which several platforms are employed for the various scenes without elaborate scenery or set changes permits the action of the play to flow swiftly from scene to scene.

Salom continued his line of serious drama with *La playa vacia* (The Empty Beach, 1970), a dark, symbolic work concerned with the struggle of a woman (Victoria) whose youth is behind her and who fights the approach of loneliness and death by first turning to sensual pleasures with a beach boy employed in her hotel. Death appears in the form of a young girl called Tana (from Thanatos)—a personification that the critic Lorenzo López Sancho called "Rilkean," noting that she came from within the character of Victoria herself and not from outside in the manner of Casona's "La Peregrina."[23] For all its elaborate symbolism, *The Enpty Beach* is never ponderous and has the power to capture the interest of audiences that may not be totally appreciative of the metaphysical intent of the play.

Viaje en un trapecio (Trip on a Trapeze, 1970) is a far lighter work than the two plays by Salom that immediately preceded it, but with all its elements of farce it is nevertheless a play of serious intent that goes beyond *The Trunk of Disguises* in the integration of popular music hall skits and circus routines into its nonrealistic development. With *La noche de los cien pájaros* (The Night of the Hundred Birds, 1972), the dramatist produced still another substantial drama to enhance his growing reputation. The play deals with the dissatisfactions of a middle-aged man whose intellectual aspirations have been frustrated because of his marriage to an attractive but commonplace woman. He is driven to the point of plotting her death only to discover the emptiness of the alternatives to his present life. Structurally it is Salom's most complex work, and the action zigzags in time with compelling dramatic effect. A comparison of the most recent works of this playwright and his conventional theatrical efforts of a decade ago reveals clearly the extent to which Salom has divorced himself from the stage conventions of the past in order to apply his talents in an increasingly personal and imaginative fashion.

CHAPTER 5

Conclusion

THE amount of theatrical writing that has been undertaken in Spain during the past quarter of a century is impressive by any standard of comparison. Hundreds of new works have been produced in the commercial and state-supported theaters or by experimental groups; many other plays remain unperformed for reasons ranging from the ubiquitous and erratic censorship to simple inadequacy of writing. Spain's theatrical tradition is long, and virtually all of the greatest names of Spanish literature, both past and present, have been attracted to drama even though their fame may derive from contributions to other genres. Today new writers continue to direct their energies toward dramatic creativity in impressive numbers in spite of the obstacles that may prevent their ultimate recognition.

The Spanish theater of the postwar period has had almost no effect on the course of contemporary drama outside Spain; but the neglect of fine and original dramatists such as Buero-Vallejo, Sastre, Martín Recuerda, and Gala (to cite some very obvious examples) can only be explained by the lack of translations of recent plays, lingering political prejudices, and the lack of impetus in the English-speaking world from Hispanic scholars sensitive to the plight of these playwrights and to the realities of the theatrical world in general.

An unfortunate polarization of critical opinion in Spain has also contributed to a distorted picture of the state of the theater in Madrid. In their zeal to promote a widespread renovation of the Spanish stage through a socially committed and politicized theater, certain critics have obstinately rejected a number of playwrights whose talents are far from pedestrian simply because their aesthetic aims do not correspond to those demanded by their attackers. At the same time, some more conservative theater observers have demonstrated an inexcusable negativism toward imaginative plays by new writers of unconventional vision. Dramatists who have chosen the course of combining serious and light theater to achieve some degree of personal security in the commercial arena have frequently been rated in terms of their most ephemeral efforts while their more worthwhile contributions—sometimes of a quality comparable to that of frequently performed works from the contemporary French or English theaters—have been ignored or casually dismissed. Several writers of the prewar generation, whose careers were interrupted by the civil war (López Rubio and Mihura in particular), deserve greater recognition for their efforts to maintain a level of artistic respectability against great odds in the period of revitalization which began in 1949.

A substantial part of theatrical writing in the 1950's was the product of cross-fertilization among Spain's own practicing writers of drama. The direct influence of Pirandello, Giraudoux, Anouilh, Priestley, and other foreign dramatists was obvious in the works of some of the most successful playwrights; but sometimes these influences were controlled by an individual style or viewpoint that produced works of genuine dramatic interest and originality. However, imitations and poorly disguised repetitions were not uncommon. In the 1960's several younger dramatists began to demonstrate a more direct concern for the harsher realities of Spanish society and to seek inspiration in Spain's own tradition, looking particularly to the example of Valle-Inclán. There has also been a group of playwrights (most of them far from the mainstream of Spanish theater) who have shown their tenacity and courage by writing in an independent vein in spite of a lack of possibilities for the actual presentation of their individualisitic creations. But these writers—Ruibal, Martínez Ballesteros, Juan M. de la Vega, and others—are beginning to emerge from obscurity, and their plays are being disseminated extensively in printed form.

In the total picture, Buero-Vallejo can now be seen as the single most important voice in the postwar theater. Belatedly, he now stands on the threshold of international fame as the plays of his maturity are finding stages throughout eastern Europe and, in a limited way, in the English-speaking world. Sastre remains a unique figure whose career has been virtually suspended as far as production of his works is concerned—a committed talent that has been lamentably shackled in his native land.

How long censorial restraints will endure in Spain is totally unpredictable. Equally uncertain are the directions of the careers of the promising writers of the 1960's and early 1970's who have found a tentative place in the contemporary theater. The potential of Gala, Martín Recuerda, Juan Antonio Castro, Diego Salvador, and Bellido has been clearly demonstrated, and it seems highly probable that one or more of them (or a dramatist still unperformed) will succeed in exerting a significant influence on theater outside the limits of the Iberian peninsula.

Notes and References

Chapter One

1. A more detailed and politically oriented account of the resumption of theatrical activity in Spain during the period of World War II can be found in *Treinta años de teatro de la derecha* (Barcelona: Tusquets Editor, 1971), by the outspoken Spanish critic José Monleón.

2. For Jardiel Poncela, see the forthcoming Twayne volume on him by Douglas McKay.

3. Both *En la ardiente oscuridad* and the first version of *Aventura en lo gris* were written before the premiere of *Historia de una escalera*. *En la ardiente oscuridad* was also an entry in the Lope de Vega competition of 1949, along with dozens of plays by other writers.

4. Arturo del Hoyo, "Sobre *Historia de una escalera*," *Insula* 4, no. 47 (November 15, 1949), 1.

5. Detailed accounts of Sastre's unperformed and unpublished plays can be found in Farris Anderson's *Alfonso Sastre* (New York: Twayne, 1971).

6. Anthony M. Pasquariello, "Alfonso Sastre: dramatist with a mission." Introduction to college text edition of *Escuadra hacia la muerte* (New York: Appleton-Century-Crofts, 1967), p. 1.

7. *Celos del aire* is a title that does not translate easily into English. It is derived from the name of a *comedia* by Calderón, *Celos aun del aire matan*—loosely: "Even imaginary jealousy can kill." *Jealous of the Air* would be a serviceable but not definitive English title. When the play was produced in Italy, the title was completely altered to *Due più due, sei* (Two Plus Two Make Six).

8. Ionesco's analysis of *Three Top Hats*, "La desmixtificación por el humor negro," can be found in Spanish in the volume dedicated to Mihura in the *Primer Acto* drama series, *Miguel Mihura*, (Madrid: Taurus Ediciones, 1965), pp. 93-95.

9. The influence of Buero's historical dramas on Casona's final play is noted by Joelyn Ruple in her *Antonio Buero Vallejo: The First Fifteen Years* (New York: Eliseo Torres & Sons, 1971), p. 15.

10. Max Aub left Spain during the civil war and spent his mature years in Mexico as an exile.

11. Francisco Ruiz Ramón, *Historia del teatro español: Siglo XX* (Madrid: Alianza Editorial, 1971), p. 469.

12. For the complete text in Spanish of Casona's letter of encouragement to Gala see "Carta a Antonio Gala," *Primer Acto*, No. 51 (1964), pp. 29-30.

13. Arrabal was actually born in Melilla (formerly Spanish Morocco) and was educated in Spain proper. At the age of twenty-two he departed for France.

14. "Correspondencia de Fernando Arrabal con J. M.," included in *Fernando Arrabal*, Colección Primer Acto 5 (Madrid: Taurus Ediciones, 1965), p. 40.

15. *Ibid.*, pp. 40-41.

16. José Monleón "Los hombres del triciclo," *Fernando Arrabal*, Colección Primer Acto 5, p. 9.

17. For a presentation of Arrabal's recent career, including his acceptance in the United States, see Charles Marowitz's article, "Arrabal's Theater of Panic," *The New York Times Magazine* (December 3, 1971), pp. 40-41, 75-106.

18. Although Prego received the Lope de Vega Award for 1963, his play was not produced until February, 1965.

19. In 1972 Bellido moved out of the "underground" category with the successful production of his full-length comedy *Milagro en Londres* (Miracle in London). In March, 1973, his drama of terrorism, *Legras negras en los Andes* (Black Letters on the Andes) had its premiere.

20. "Tres autores marginados," *Primer Acto*, no. 123-24 (Aug.-Sept. 1970), 48-49.

21. The Lady Pepa opened in February, 1969, with *El viudo* (The Widower) by Carmen Llorca. By 1973 there were nine *cafés-teatro* in Madrid and five in Barcelona. The concept of *café-teatro* is actually not new. In an article in *Mundo Hispánico*, no. 287 (February 1972), pp. 27-31, Alfredo Marqueríe has pointed out that similar intimate theaters flourished in Madrid in the nineteenth century between 1860 and 1890.

22. The name of Manuel Parada is closely associated with music for the contemporary Spanish stage. He has provided incidental material for such works as Ruiz Iriarte's *El carrusell* and *Un paraguas bajo la lluvia* and Buero's *La tejedora de sueños* and *Irene o el tesoro*, as well as complete scores.

23. One of Buero-Vallejo's most intriguing works, *Mito* (Myth), was written to serve as an opera libretto for the composer Cristóbal Halffner; but the score (if completed) has not been performed.

24. The Teatro Real, Madrid's Opera House, was damaged during bombardments of the civil war. Although the Real has been restored, it has become a concert hall and the full stage facilities are not operational. Opera productions are now staged at the well-equipped Teatro de la

Zarzuela. Madrid's opera season in the late spring is brief and does not compare with the more important season of the Liceo in Barcelona.

25. This figure includes the *cafés-teatro* and several variety houses where popular artists and a vaudeville-type of entertainment are presented.

26. For a more detailed presentation of the economics of Spain's theater, see Luis Molero Manglano's article, "Economic, Social and Cultural Aspects of the Theatre," *Spain Today*, no. 3 (June 1970), pp. 57-62.

27. Marsillach is probably the most versatile actor of his generation. As a juvenile performer, he created the role of Ignacio in Buero's *In the Burning Darkness* in 1950, and in 1961 he portrayed Hamlet in Buero's version of Shakespeare's tragedy. More recently he was highly acclaimed for his direction of the controversial Llovet version of *Tartuffe*, in which he also performed in the title role.

28. Professor O'Connor has published three articles on her investigations into censorship: "Government Censorship in the Contemporary Spanish Theater," *Educational Theater Journal* 18, no. 4 (December 1966), "Censorship in the Contemporary Spanish Theater and Antonio Buero Vallejo," *Hispania* 52, no. 2 (May 1969), and "Torquemada in the Theatre," *Theatre Survey* 14, no. 2 (November 1973). It was reported in *Hispania* 55, no. 3 (September 1972), 565, that Mrs. O'Connor had been expelled from Spain because the Spanish Foreign Ministry maintained that her research did not serve academic ends. However, after a protest from the United States government, the Spanish authorities offered the scholar reimbursement for her travel expenses and invited her to resume her investigations.

29. The original version of *Aventura en lo gris* (Adventure in Grayness) appeared in *Teatro*, no. 10 (January-February-March 1954); the "definitive" version is available in Collección Teatro, no. 408, and in Isabel Magaña Schevill's textbook edition of the play (New York: Appleton-Century,Crofts, 1967).

30. O'Connor, "Censorship . . . and Buero Vallejo," p. 282.

31. Angel Gómez Escorial, "Minucioso Buero," *Blanco y Negro*, no. 3131 (May 6, 1972), pp. 38-39. A year after the publication of this interview, Buero's newest play, *La fundación* (The Foundation) was encountering serious difficulties with the censors. It was finally performed in January, 1974.

32. Gómez Escorial, "La noche de Alonso Millán," *Blanco y Negro*, no. 3134 (May 27, 1972), p. 37.

33. Charles Marowitz, "Theater in London: Malcolm and Macduff Escape Into Swaziland," *The New York Times*, Section 2 (May 7, 1972), p. 1. The entry from Spain discussed by Mr. Marowitz was the Victor García-Nuria Espert production of *Yerma* later seen in New York.

Chapter Two

1. *Un hombre de bien* and *El año 2.550* were listed as works "unpublished and repudiated" by Jardiel Poncela in "La obra teatral de Enrique Jardiel Poncela," *Teatro*, no. 4 (February 1953), pp. 37-44.

2. *Al fin sola* was performed as *Su mano derecha* and published in the collection "La Farsa," no. 20 (January 21, 1928) under the name of Honorio Maura.

3. *Overnight* was performed in England as *Max and Mr. Max* in a translation by Cecil Madden.

4. Carlos Fernández Cuenca, "El autor y su obra preferida," *Correo Literario* 3, no. 62 (December 15, 1952), 12.

5. Review in *Escorial* 19, no. 57 (1949), 420.

6. *Alberto*, Colección Teatro, no. 30 (Madrid: Escelicer, 1952), p. 28.

7. *Ibid.*, p. 84.

8. Gonzalo Torrente Ballester, "Crónica de teatros," *Escorial* 21, no. 65 (January-February 1950), 224.

9. Theodore S. Beardsley, Jr., "The Illogical Character in Contemporary Spanish Drama," *Hispania* 41 (December 1958), 447.

10. *Celos del aire*, Colección Teatro, no. 2 (Madrid: Escelicer, 1951), p. 34.

11. *Ibid.*, p. 75.

12. Alfredo Marquerie, *Veinte años de teatro en España* (Madrid: Editora Nacional, 1959), p. 110.

13. *Cena de Navidad*, Colección Teatro, no. 7 (Madrid: Escelicer, 1952), pp. 49-50.

14. Federico Sainz de Robles, *introduction to* Teatro, español, 1951-52 (Madrid: Aguilar, 1952), p. 12.

15. Noted in "El autor y su obra preferida," p. 12.

16. Reported by Rafael Vásquez Zamora, "Teatro," *Insula* 9, no. 102 (June 1, 1954), 12.

17. Angel Valbuena Prat, *Historia del teatro español* (Barcelona: Editorial Noguer, 1956), p. 672.

18. Reported by David Menor, "Teatro: el tema y la manera," *Ateneo*, no. 23 (November 6, 1952), p. 20.

19. *El remedio en la memoria*, Colección Teatro, no. 48 (Madrid: Escelicer, 1952), pp. 11-12.

20. One thinks particularly of the case of Merche in Jardiel's *Los tigres escondidos en la alcoba*.

21. Unmistakable examples of Pirandellian influence in López Rubio's theater are the role-playing of Germán, which brings to mind Pirandello's *Come tu mi vuoi*, and the flamboyant "roles" of Aunt Carolina.

22. Review reprinted in Sainz de Robles, *Teatro español, 1954-55*, p. 261.

23. Reprinted from *Triunfo*, in Sainz, *Teatro español, 1958-59*, pp. 3-4.

24. Eusebio García-Luengo, "*Las manos son inocentes*," *Indice* 3, no. 119 (November 1958), 19.

25. Celestino Martí Farreras, "*Las manos son inocentes*," *Destino* 23, no. 1155 (September 26, 1959), 46.

26. Colección Teatro, no. 272, p. 74.

27. López Rubio permitted the writer to read the manuscript of *The Way of the Angel* in Spain in June, 1971.

28. *A B C* (Edición semanal aérea), April 6, 1972, p. 11.

29. Reprinted in *Miguel Mihura*, Colección Primer Acto (Madrid: Taurus Ediciones, 1965), pp. 9-29.

30. *Ibid.*, p. 10.

31. Reprinted in Sainz, *Teatro español, 1952-53*, p. 91.

32. Translated by Marcia C. Wellwarth, in *Modern Spanish Theater* (New York: E. P. Dutton, 1969), pp. 185-86.

33. John V. Falconieri and Anthony M. Pasquariello, *Mi adorado Juan* (New York: Blaisdell, 1964), p. xv.

34. Monleón, *Treinta años de teatro de la derecha* (Barcelona: Tusquets Editor, 1971), p. 88.

35. Falconieri and Pasquariello, *Mi adorado Juan*, p. xiv.

36. Edith B. Sublette, *Carlota* (New York: The Odyssey Press, 1963), p. xi.

37. Marquerie, *Veinte años de teatro en España*, p. 153.

38. *La bella Dorotea*, in Sainz, *Teatro español, 1963-64* (Madrid: Aguilar, 1965), pp. 53-54.

39. Reprinted in *Teatro español, 1963-64*, p. 34.

40. *La bella Dorotea*, p. 90.

41. Lorenzo López Sancho, "*Sólo el amor y la luna traen fortuna* de Mihura, en la Comedia," *A B C* , Sept, 12, 1968, p. 75.

42. For a detailed commentary on illogical humor in the plays of Mihura and other contemporary dramatists, see Phyllis Z. Boring's article, "Incongruous Humor in the Contemporary Spanish Theater," *Modern Drama* II, no. 1 (May 1968), 82-86.

43. Review by José María Junyet for *El Correo Catalán*, reprinted in *Teatro español, 1950-51* (Madrid: Aguilar, 1957), p. 383.

44. *Criminal de guerra*, in Sainz, *Teatro español, 1950-51*, p. 445.

45. Gonzalo Torrente Ballester, *Teatro español contemporáneo* (Madrid: Ediciones Guadarrama, 1957), pp. 302-04.

46. *Historia del teatro español*, pp. 674-75.

47. *Teatro español contemporáneo*, p. 305.

48. *Historia del teatro español: Siglo XX*, p. 347.

49. Sainz, *Teatro español, 1954-55* (Madrid: Aguilar, 1956), pp. 97-118.

50. Monleón, *Treinta años de teatro de la derecha*, p. 94.

51. Jerónimo Mallo, "La muralla y su éxito en el teatro español contemporáneo," *Hispania* 45, no. 3 (Sept. 1962), 383-88.

52. Sainz, Introduction to *Teatro español, 1956-57* (Madrid: Aguilar, 1958), pp. 56-57.

53. We may also assume that Calvo-Sotelo was familiar with several contemporary historical plays on religious figures from other countries, such as Osborne's *Luther* and Anouilh's *Beckett, ou l'honneur de Dieu*.

54. *El inocente*, in Sainz, *Teatro español, 1968-69* (Madrid: Aguilar, 1970), p. 111.

55. *Ibid.*, p. 123.

56. *Ibid.*, pp. 152-53.

57. Both Alfredo Marquerie *(Pueblo)* and Rafael García Serrano *(El Alcázar)* use the term "tragicomedia" in their reviews which are reprinted in *Teatro español, 1968-69*.

58. *Teatro español*, 1968-69, p. 73.

59. *Historia del teatro español, Siglo XX*, p. 346.

60. Phyllis Z. Boring has noted the influence of Giraudoux in Pemán's *Electra* in her article "Traces of Giraudoux in the Contemporary Spanish Theater," *Romance Notes* 11 (1969), 8-11.

61. William Giuliano, *Buero Vallejo, Sastre, y el teatro de su tiempo* (New York: Las Américas, 1971), p. 20.

62. This play was inspired by Ramón Solís's novel *Los que no tienen paz (Those Who Have No Peace)*, but the title has a different origin. In his *autocrítica*, the author writes: "I took the strange title of this work from a primitive legend that they told me in Panamá, where some monkeys in a cage in the hotel garden could be heard screeching at sunrise. According to the legend, God promised the monkeys that he would turn them into men at dawn. Since then, each time it dawns, the monkeys cry out for the fulfillment of the divine promise. It seems to me an image of the cry with which man, ever since reason began to grow in him, has asked to overcome his misery and to obtain something beyond his reach." (Colección Teatro, no. 419, p. 5.)

63. *Tres testigos*, in Sainz, *Teatro español, 1969-70* (Madrid: Aguilar, 1971), p. 300.

64. *Ibid.*, p. 301.

75. Nuñez, "*Tres testigos* de José María Pemán," *Domingos de A B C*, May 10, 1970, p. 18.

66. *Ibid.*, 19-20.

67. Torrente, *Teatro español contemporáneo*, p. 282.

68. Both Luca de Tena and his character are unaware that the

feminine version of the name in English is "Frances" and not "Francis." In fact, Francis Grey remarks in the play that the masculine and feminine forms are identical.

69. *¿Dónde vas, Alfonso XII?*, Colección Teatro, no. 209 (Madrid: Escelicer, 1959), p. 49.

70. In her article "Luca de Tena, Pirandello, and the Spanish Tradition," *Hispania* 50, no. 2 (May 1967), Wilma Newberry has provided an exceptionally perceptive study of the multiple and sometimes inseparable influences of Pirandello, Unamuno, and the nineteenth-century dramatists Tamayo y Baus and Echegaray on Luca de Tena's *¿Quién soy yo?*, *Yo soy Brandel*, and his *De lo pintado a lo vivo* (1944). She lays the groundwork for further investigations into the important interrelationships in the Spanish and Italian theater (which will eventually have to consider currents reaching Spain via the neo-Pirandellian drama of France).

71. *Prólogo* to *Teatro selecto de Edgar Neville* (Madrid: Escelicer, 1968), pp. 5-11. In this sensitively written tribute to Neville, Ruiz Iriarte not only gives us insight into the personality of this unusual artist but also provides a view of the intellectual ferment that had begun in Madrid on the eve of the Second Republic.

Chapter Three

1. From an interview with Julio Trenas, "Víctor Ruiz Iriarte, Presidente de la S.G.A.E.," *A B C*, July 22, 1969.

2. *El landó de seis caballos*, Colección Teatro, no. 80 (Madrid: Escelicer, 1953), pp. 60-61.

3. *Ibid.*, p. 66.

4. *Ibid.*, p. 67.

5. Phyllis Z. Boring, "Traces of Giraudoux in the Contemporary Spanish Theater," *Romance Notes* 11 (1969), 9-10.

6. Gerald E. Wade, "The Comedies of Víctor Ruiz Iriarte," *Hispania* 45, no. 4 (December 1962), 705.

7. "*Juego de niños*" translates into English literally as "A Children's Game," but I have elected to use the title suggested by Isabel Magaña Schevill in her excellent textbook edition of the play.

8. One may assume that Ruiz Iriarte intentionally borrowed the name "Candida" from George Bernard Shaw's play of that title.

9. *El pobrecito embustero*, in *Teatro español, 1952-53* (Madrid: Aguilar, 1954), p. 319.

10. *Ibid.*, p. 349.

11. Review by A. Rodríguez de León, from *España* (Tangiers), reprinted in *Teatro español, 1952-53*, p. 300.

12. *El carrusell*, Colección Teatro, no. 457 (Madrid: Escelicer, 1965), p. 15.

13. *Ibid.*, pp. 88-89.

14. "Nota del autor," *El carrusell* (New York: Appleton-Century-Crofts, 1970), pp. xix,xx.

15. For example, William Giuliano, in his *Buero Vallejo, Sastre y el teatro de su tiempo*, analyzes a number of Ruiz Iriarte's plays but does not include the three serious works of the 1960's discussed in the present study. Although Isabel Magaña Schevill's introduction to her textbook edition of *Juego de niños* was written before the publication of several of Ruiz Iriarte's most important works, the presentation is a sensitive discussion of the essence of this playwright's theater.

16. Francisco García Pavón, *El teatro social en España (1895-1962)* (Madrid: Taurus Ediciones, 1962), pp. 138-39.

17. In the ineffective adaptation for the screen, the action of *Story of a Stairway* is opened up to include scenes both in the city and inside the apartments. Consequently, the symbolic importance of the stairway is minimized. At the end, the young lovers are seen running hand-in-hand through the streets of Madrid toward an implied happy existence.

18. From this writer's unpublished translation of *En la ardiente oscuridad*.

19. Of the six full-length plays Buero wrote before 1953, all are in three acts except *Adventure in Grayness*, which has two acts separated by a dream sequence.

20. An English version by William Oliver appears in Robert Corrigan's *Masterpieces of Modern Spanish Theatre* (New York: Collier Books, 1967).

21. Joelyn Ruple, *Antonio Buero Vallejo: The First Fifteen Years* (New York: Eliseo Torres & Sons, 1971), p. 94.

22. The nature of the rewriting is elaborated on in Buero's own commentary that follows the published text of the play (Colección Teatro, no. 21, p. 66).

23. Colección Teatro, no. 21, p. 67.

24. Martha Halsey, *Antonio Buero Vallejo* (New York: Twayne, 1973), pp. 59-62.

25. *Ibid.*, p. 60.

26. "Comentario," *Hoy es fiesta*, Colección Teatro, no. 176 (Madrid: Escelicer, 1957), p. 108.

27. *Antonio Buero Vallejo*, p. 71.

28. *Las Meninas*, Colección Teatro, no. 285 (Madrid: Escelicer, 1961), p. 72.

29. From Farris Anderson's translation in *The Modern Spanish Stage: Four Plays* (New York: Hill & Wang, 1970), pp. 137-38.

30. Robert L. Nicholas, *The Tragic Stages of Antonio Buero Vallejo* (Chapel Hill: Estudios de Hispanófila, 1972), p. 72.

31. Review from *La Estafeta Literaria* reprinted in *Teatro español, 1962-63* (Madrid: Aguilar, 1963), p. 75.

32. Review from *Triunfo* reprinted in *Teatro español, 1962-63*, p. 78.

33. *Buero Vallejo, Sastre y el teatro de su tiempo*, p. 14.

34. The libretto was originally intended for the composer Cristóbal Halffter.

35. For a complete presentation of the use of projections in *The Sleep of Reason*, see John Dowling's important article, "Buero Vallejo's Interpretation of Goya's 'Black Paintings,'" *Hispania* 56, no. 2 (May 1973), 449-57.

36. *El sueño de la razón*, in *Teatro español, 1969-70* ((Madrid: Aguilar, 1971), p. 215.

37. From this writer's unpublished translation of *La llegada de los dioses*. The original Spanish of Veronica's reply is: "¡Moriremos caminando!"

38. No doubt the fact that some of the characters appeared onstage in a state of seminudity contributed to the box office success of the play.

39. "Sobre *Llegada de los dioses*, una entrevista con Antonio Buero Vallejo," *Primer acto*, no. 138 (November 1971), pp. 27-38.

40. *Ibid.*

41. On March 9, 1973, this writer considered Buero's alienated visionaries in a paper delivered at the Conference on Twentieth Century Literature, University of Louisville.

42. For detailed considerations of the visual, musical, and symbolic features of Buero's plays, see both Robert L. Nicholas's *The Tragic Stages of Antonio Buero Vallejo* (Chapel Hill: Estudios de Hispanófila, 1972) and José Ramón Cortina's *El arte dramático de Antonio Buero Vallejo* (Madrid: Editorial Gredos, 1969).

43. For a detailed presentation of Buero-Vallejo's theories of tragedy, see Kessel Schwartz's "Buero Vallejo and the Concept of Tragedy," *Hispania* 51, no. 4 (December 1968), 817-24, Martha T. Halsey's "Buero Vallejo and the Significance of Hope," *Hispania* 51, no. 1 (March 1968), 57-66, and Halsey's *Antonio Buero Vallejo* (New York: Twayne, 1973).

44. García Pavón, "Se estrenó *La fundación* de Antonio Buero Vallejo," *Blanco y Negro*, no. 3221 (January 26, 1974), p. 70.

45. Farris Anderson, *Alfonso Sastre* (New York: Twayne, 1971), pp. 17-18.

46. *Historia del teatro español, Siglo XX*, p. 450.

47. "Autocrítica" of *La cornada*, in Sainz, *Teatro español, 1959-* (Madrid: Aguilar, 1961), p. 163.

48. *Historia del teatro español, Siglo XX*, p. 446.

49. Anderson, *Alfonso Sastre*, pp. 102-106.

50. "Nota del autor," *Teatro español, 1966-67* (Madrid: Aguilar, 1968), p. 91.

51. *Alfonso Sastre*, p. 70.

52. *Ibid., p. 71.*

53. For information on the plot, structure, and characteristics of the four unpublished "epic" plays, this writer has relied entirely on Farris Anderson's detailed study based on the original manuscripts.

54. Sastre's *Ana Kleiber*—a work unlikely to establish a reputation for him at best—was performed in English off-Broadway in 1965 in a distressingly melodramatic production. The staging of *Escuadra hacia la muerte* in Spanish in 1973 by an off off-Broadway group did not reach an English-speaking audience, and although reception of the production was favorable, the play was not admired by those who reviewed it. *Death Thrust* has been performed in Texas.

55. Paso and his wife are now separated.

56. Review from *A B C*, reprinted in *Teatro español, 1959-60* (Madrid: Aguilar, 1961), p. 232.

57. Alfredo Marqueñe, *Alfonso Paso y su teatro* (Madrid: Escelicer, 1960), pp. 173-74.

58. "Cinco puntualizaciones," *Teatro selecto de Alfonso Paso* (Madrid: Escelicer, 1971), p. 61.

59. *Teatro social en España*, p. 172.

60. Obviously this title is Paso's own comment on Peter Weiss's title for the play generally known as *Marat-Sade*.

61. It could be demonstrated that Paso intends Rome to represent the United States (or New York City). One interesting line reads: ". . . Rome has killed the song of the cicada." (episode 2). Not long before the composition of the play, a production of Paso's *El canto de la cigarra* (The Song of the Cicada) with the word "cigarra" mistranslated as "grasshopper" had been an utter flop on Broadway.

62. Lorenzo López Sancho, "Estreno de *Nerón-Paso* en el Reina Victoria," *A B C*, September 7, 1969, pp. 65-66.

63. "Cinco puntualizaciones," *Teatro selecto*, p. 80.

64. *Teatro selecto de Alfonso Paso*, p. 492.

Chapter Four

1. Domingo Pérez Minik, *Teatro europeo contemporáneo* (Madrid: Ediciones Guadarrama, 1961), pp. 485-87.

2. *El tintero*, Colección Teatro, no. 353 (Madrid: Escelicer, 1962), p. 8.

3. For a commentary on the use of sound in Muñiz's theater, see

Angelo A. Borras's article, "Sound, Music and Symbolism in Carlos Muñiz's Theatre," *Romance Notes* 12 (1970), 31-35.

4. Colección Teatro, no. 353, p. 95.

5. *Teatro social en España*, p. 152.

6. *Historia del teatro español, Siglo XX*, pp. 478-79.

7. Review from *Arriba*, reprinted in *Teatro Español, 1961-62* (Madrid: Aguilar, 1963), pp. 170-171.

8. *Historia del teatro español, Siglo XX*, p. 479.

9. *El charlatán*, Colección Teatro, no. 396 (Madrid: Escelicer, 1963), p. 44.

10. The original title of the work is in English.

11. *El teatrito de don Ramón*, Colección Teatro, no. 642 (Madrid: Escelicer, 1969), p. 13.

12. *Ibid.*, p. 66.

13. Review from *A B C*, reprinted in *José Martín Recuerda* (Madrid: Taurus Ediciones, 1969), p. 68.

14. Comment by Domenech reprinted in *José Martín Recuerda*, p. 69.

15. *Historia del teatro español, Siglo XX*, p. 482.

16. "Pequeñas memories," included in *José Martín Recuerda*, p. 55.

17. *Ibid.*, p. 57.

18. The play was originally called *La maestra* (The Teacher).

19. Sastre was twenty-seven when *Escuadra hacia la muerte* was presented, but the work was performed by an experimental group and was a success only in terms of the controversy that surrounded it. Gala's play was given a major production.

20. "Autocrítica" reprinted in *Teatro español, 1963-64* (Madrid: Aguilar, 1965), p. 183.

21. "Antonio Gala: Un Gulliver del teatro español," *S P*, no. 278 (January 23, 1966), p. 54.

22. Reprinted in *Teatro español, 1967-68* (Madrid: Aguilar, 1969), p. 239.

23. Review from *A B C*, reprinted in *Teatro español, 1970-71* (Madrid: Aguilar, 1972), p. 160.

Selected Bibliography

PRIMARY SOURCES

1. In English

BENEDIKT, MICHAEL, and WELLWARTH, GEORGE E. *Modern Spanish Theatre*. (New York: E. P. Dutton & Co., 1969). Translations of plays by Mihura, Casona, Olmo, Arrabal, Bellido, and earlier dramatists, with excellent biographical and critical introductory material.

CORRIGAN, ROBERT W. *Masterpieces of the Modern Spanish Theatre*. (New York: Collier Books, 1967). Translations of Buero's *La tejedora de sueños* and Sastre's *La cornada*, as well as works by earlier dramatists. The biographical material is inadequate and sometimes inaccurate; the introduction is not recommended.

HOLT, MARION. *The Modern Spanish Stage: Four Plays*. (New York: Hill & Wang, 1970). Translations of plays by Buero-Vallejo, Sastre, López Rubio, and Casona, with an informative critical introduction to Spain's postwar theater.

WELLWARTH, GEORGE E. *The New Wave Spanish Drama*. (New York: New York University Press, 1970). Translations of plays by Sastre, Ruibal, Bellido, and Martínez Ballesteros, with a critical introduction.

Note. Some of the translations in the collections listed above first appeared in *Modern International Drama*, a journal which continues to provide a unique service in publishing acceptable English translations of plays by contemporary European dramatists.

2. In Spanish

The yearly anthology of plays selected by Federico Sainz de Robles and published by Aguilar in Madrid offers five or six representative works of every theatrical season from 1949-50 to the present, as well as selected reviews, the authors' *autocríticas*, and a complete documentation of premieres, awards, and other matters pertaining to the theater of Spain.

More than six hundred titles have been published in the Colección teatro of Escelicer since 1949. A large percentage of the works in this inexpensive series represents contemporary Spanish playwrights.

Under the editorship of José Monleón, Taurus Ediciones, Madrid, has published a series of inexpensive anthologies (with critical articles and biographical data) dedicated to the works of individual playwrights. Buero-Vallejo, Sastre, Mihura, Muñiz, Martín Recuerda, Gala, Rodríguez Mendez, and others are included in the series.

Primer acto, a monthly drama journal of staunchly independent editorial policy, publishes either a new Spanish play or the translation of a contemporary foreign drama in each issue.

SECONDARY SOURCES

1. In English

ANDERSON, FARRIS. *Alfonso Sastre.* (New York: Tawyne, 1971). A highly recommended study of Sastre's plays and other writings by a leading authority on this dramatist in the United States.

BORING, PHYLLIS Z. "Incongruous Humor in the Contemporary Spanish Theater." *Modern Drama* II, 1 (May 1969), 82-86. A brief look at a little-explored but essential aspect of contemporary Spanish theater. The author deals specifically with examples from plays of Jardiel Poncela, Mihura, and Paso.

————. "Traces of Giraudoux in the Contemporary Spanish Theatre." *Romance Notes* 11 (1969), 8-11. A brief look at another subject that invites further exploration.

BORRAS, ANGELO A. "Sound, Music and Symbolism in Carlos Muñiz's Theatre." *Romance Notes* 12 (1970), 31-35. A perceptive article on an important aspect of Muñiz's plays.

DOWLING, JOHN. "Buero Vallejo's Interpretation of Goya's 'Black Painting.' " *Hispania* 56, no. 2 (May 1973), 449-57. Highly recommended as background for reading (or staging) *El Sueño de la razón,* one of Buero's finest dramas. Without explanation this splendid study turned up under "Fact and Opinion" in the pages of *Hispania.*

HALSEY, MARTHA T. "Buero Vallejo and the Significance of Hope," *Hispania.* 51 no. 1 (March 1969), 57-65. One of the best of Halsey's several articles on Buero and a lucid explanation of the playwright's theories of tragedy.

————. *Antonio Buero Vallejo.* (New York: Tawyne, 1973). The most thorough presentation to date of Buero's thought and his development as a playwright from his first plays through *El sueño de la razón.* Recommended.

HOLT, MARION P. "López Rubio's Venture into Serious Drama." *Hispania* 49, no. 4 (Dec. 1966), 764-68. A detailed study of López Rubio's atypical drama *Las manos son inocentes*.

————. "López Rubio's *Alberto:* Character Revelation and Form. *Modern Drama* 10, no. 2 (Sept. 1967), 144-50. A study of the structure of the playwright's first contribution to the postwar theater.

NEWBERRY, WILMA. "Luca de Tena, Pirandello, and the Spanish Tradition." *Hispania* 50, no. 2 (May 1967), 253-61. An introduction to a complex and important aspect of Spanish theater by a perceptive critic.

NICHOLAS, ROBERT L. *The Tragic Stages of Antonio Buero Vallejo.* (Chapel Hill: Estudios de Hispanófila, University of North Carolina, 1972). This recommended study is principally concerned with the symbolic, visual, and technical aspects of Buero's theater.

O'CONNOR, PATRICIA W. "Censorship in the Contemporary Spanish Theater and Antonio Buero Vallejo." *Hispania* 52, no. 2 (May 1969), 282-88. Recommended. The author is the best-informed scholar in the United States on the complex nature of Spanish censorship.

————. "Torquemada in the Theatre." *Theatre Survey* 14, no. 2 (Nov. 1973), 33-45. Further observations on the problem of censorship, with reference to the difficulties of Muñiz, Olmo, and others.

RUPLE, JOELYN *Antonio Buero Vallejo: The First Fifteen Years.* (New York: Eliseo Torres & Sons, 1971). This first study to appear in English on Buero's theater is a sensitive and highly readable introduction to a major dramatist.

SCHEVILL, ISABEL MAGAÑA. Introduction to *Juego de niños.* (Englewood Cliffs, N.J.: Prentice-Hall, 1965), viii-xxii. Although written before the appearance of several of Ruiz Iriarte's best plays, this is an excellent introduction to the themes and dramatic techniques of this playwright.

WADE, GERALD E. "The Comedies of Víctor Ruiz Iriarte." *Hispania* 45, no. 4 (Dec. 1962), 704-11. A consideration of the playwright's earlier plays, with interesting observations on the nature of comedy.

WELLWARTH, GEORGE E. *Spanish Underground Drama.* (University Park: The Pennsylvania State University Press, 1972). A presentation of the writings of a number of marginal playwrights (dubbed "underground dramatists" by Wellwarth himself). While one may disagree with some of the author's evaluations, the total effort is praiseworthy. An essential work for an understanding of a special area of creativity in Spain.

2. In Spanish

CARBALLO, J. ROF. *et al. El teatro de humor en España.* (Madrid:

Editora Nacional, 1966). Articles by various writers on the nature of humor in the modern Spanish theater. Not all are of equal interest. Recommended.

CORTINA, JOSE RAMÓN. *El arte dramático de Antonio Buero Vallejo.* (Madrid: Editorial Gredos, 1969). An excellent presentation of the symbolic and scenic elements of Buero's theater.

GARCIA PAVON, FRANCISCO. *Teatro social en España.* (Madrid: Taurus, 1962). This study deals with the entire twentieth-century Spanish theater; the writers from the contemporary period considered are Buero, Sastre, Muñiz, and Paso.

GIULIANO, WILLIAM. *Buero Vallejo, Sastre y el teatro de su tiempo.* (New York: Las Americas, 1971). As the title suggests, this work is most detailed in the sections on Buero and Sastre. The works of all the writers who began to contribute to the Spanish theater prior to the appearance of Buero and Sastre are treated as "teatro de diversión"—a label that is not wholly applicable to the diverse works produced by these dramatists.

MARQUERIE, ALFREDO. *Veinte años de teatro en España.* (Madrid: Editora Nacional, 1959). Although it does not deal with the theater of the 1960's, this is a useful work for material and opinions on a number of works that were not published or which are difficult to obtain.

———. *Alfonso Paso y su teatro.* (Madrid: Escelicer, 1960). An interesting study of Paso's creative approach, relationships to other playwrights, and personal opinions. Based in part on personal discussions with Paso, this book is unique in its approach among existing investigations on individual writers of the contemporary period.

———. *Ensayo critico del teatro de Jaime Salom.* (Madrid: Escelicer, 1973). Marquerie's latest study and the first extended consideration of a playwright who has become increasingly prominent in recent years.

RUIZ RAMÓN, FRANCISCO. *Historia del teatro español,* vol. 2 (Madrid: Alianza Editorial, 1971). The best and most complete work in Spanish on the contemporary theater. Although one may not always agree with this scholar's judgments on individual works or writers, the documentation is exemplary and the overall view of the period is presented with unquestionable authority. Highly recommended.

TORRENTE BALLESTER, GONZALO. *Teatro español contemporáneo.* (Madrid: Ediciones Guadarrama, 1957). Long a standard critical work on the modern Spanish theater. The sections devoted to the postwar period are based largely on reviews of plays which the author wrote over a period of years.

Index